THE RIGHT TO
BE YOURSELF

THE RIGHT TO BE YOURSELF

How to be assertive and make changes in your life

TOBE ALEKSANDER

PIATKUS

First published in 1992 by
Judy Piatkus (Publishers) Ltd
5 Windmill Street, London W1P 1HF

The moral right of the author has been asserted

*A catalogue record for this book is available from
the British Library*

ISBN 0-7499-1144-1

Designed by Sue Ryall

Typeset in Compugraphic Times by
Action Typesetting Ltd, Gloucester
Printed and bound in Great Britain by
Biddles Ltd, Guildford and King's Lynn

For Peggy and Mick, with love and thanks

Contents

Introduction

Are you happy? Are you fulfilled? Are you who you want to be?

For many women, daily existence is reduced to a process of simply getting by – keeping a relationship going, looking after the kids, caring for parents, putting in the required hours at work, holding the family together. The constant need to care, nurture, put others first, can seriously dent your self-esteem and put an obstacle in the way of achieving your self-potential. There simply isn't the time or room to create personal space; or any opportunity to stop and consider the next move in the game of life.

What about you? Are you trapped in a glass prison looking out? Do you watch life pass you by and wish you were part of it? Do you harbour secret ambitions and fantasise about how things could be, if only ...? Do you inhabit a world of missed opportunities? Who's in charge of your life – you or your circumstances? Perhaps it's time to break the routine. To stop being at everyone else's beck and call. To say what you think, stand up for what you believe and put yourself first.

It doesn't matter who you are, what you do or what your situation is; you *can* make changes in your life. You can cut out the dead wood, discover new horizons and make things happen for you. So how do you make the first move?

The key to taking charge of your destiny is to become assertive. To develop that deep-down belief in yourself, to have

1

the confidence to decide what it is you want — and to go for it! This book is about helping you to develop that self-belief and equipping you with the skills to go out and make changes.

Chapter 1 explains what assertion is all about and how to recognise assertive and non-assertive behaviour. It also gives you a chance to get to know yourself a bit better and get down on paper all the things that make you tick.

Chapter 2 looks at the very basics of assertiveness. It teaches you how to think assertively, talk assertively and look assertive.

Chapter 3 goes through some essential skills you'll need to help you become more confident. It shows you how to make requests and say 'no' without feeling guilty. It also looks at how to confront difficult situations and deal with criticism. Most important of all, it explains how to write a survival script, so that you'll never be lost for words again.

Chapter 4 shows you how to be assertive in special situations like meeting people at a party, going for an interview, making a presentation or enjoying sex.

Chapter 5 is a quiz to help you check up on your assertion know-how so far.

Chapter 6 looks at fourteen everyday situations from dealing with teenagers to talking to your doctor, asking for a pay rise to coping with an interfering parent. It shows you how to find assertive solutions to some potentially thorny problems and suggests the words and actions you can use.

The final chapter is all about giving you that extra boost. Up until then we've concentrated on getting the inside right, now it's time to add the glamour from the outside! The chapter gives beauty and fashion tips, and suggests ways to manage your time effectively — and, very important, how to switch off.

So what's stopping you from taking the plunge? A fear of failing, of rejection or of fear itself? Becoming assertive will give you the confidence to take risks, accept challenges and manage your fear. Reality is never as frightening as you think. Don't wait on the sidelines for ever. Now's the time to take responsibility for your life. Make the changes you want. You've the right to be yourself.

Go on, what are you waiting for?

1

From the
Inside Out

Learning to be assertive inevitably becomes a voyage of self-discovery. Before you can start making changes in your life and become the person you really want to be, you need to begin to know yourself as you are now – warts and all.

When was the last time you sat down and thought long and hard about you? Not just the regrets and failures that all of us have experienced but your achievements, the people who are important to you, the things that make you laugh. At this moment you probably know more about your best friend's likes and dislikes than your own.

Assertion is about honesty. It means confronting the satisfaction and dissatisfaction in your life, coming to terms with those things you can't change and appreciating where you have the power to make a difference.

GETTING TO KNOW YOU

This is a totally self-indulgent exercise. It's intended as much for fun as for self-revelation, so don't feel embarrassed or guilty about completing it. Feel free to boast, to laugh, to cry. There are no right and wrong answers – just write whatever comes into your head. Write your answers on a sheet of paper.

My favourite... (You don't have to go into details!)
Place ....
Season ....
Time of day ....
Colour ....
Book ....
Music ....
Car ....
Film ....
Food ....
Clothes ....

The three things I do for pure pleasure ....

People
The people I admire most ....
The people I love most ....
Five things that really turn me off people ....
Five things that really turn me on people ....

Emotions
My greatest joys are/were ....
My biggest fears are/were ....
What makes me laugh most is ....
What upsets me most is ....
When I'm happy, I ....
When I get angry, I ....
What makes me cry, is ....
When I'm nervous, I ....
I know I feel on top of the world when ....
I know I feel down when ....

Personality and body
My three best characteristics ....
My three worst characteristics ....
My two best body features ....
My two worst body features ....
Three things I'm really good at ....
Three things I'm most proud of having achieved ....

4

Three things I feel most frustrated/angry/disappointed with myself for having or not having done ....

Dreams

My greatest ambition is ....
My biggest fantasy is ....
Describe your dream home − furnish it, decorate it, who lives there with you − how do you feel?

Describe your dream job or career − what you do, what your office looks like, your boss and your colleagues (if you have them), your salary − how do you feel?

Describe your dream holiday − where are you, what's the scenery and weather like, who's with you − how do you feel?

Imagine you have at your disposal a top fashion designer, hair stylist and make-up artist to give you a 'make over' from top to toe. What would you ask them to do? How do you feel when they've finished?

The future

Next week, I want to ....
Next month, I want to ....
Next year, I want to ....
In the next five years I want to ....

What would you most like to change about yourself − your personality, looks, family or work situation? Why? Do you think you can achieve those changes?

Well, how difficult was that? Have you left any blank spaces? Did you squirm at the questions or blush at your answers?

It's not often that we get the chance to analyse what makes us laugh and gives us pleasure. Desires and ambitions get swept under the carpet as we scurry around trying to cope with home and work commitments. When was the last time you acknowledged your accomplishments or your most attractive feature? Remember, we may not be Florence Nightingale or Madonna but we're all good at something. You don't need to have a string of letters after your name to be a sympathetic listener, an efficient organiser, a supportive friend, a cheery colleague or excellent cake-maker. And as for looks, it's all relative. Six foot tall and slender they may be, but top models still subject themselves to the surgeon's knife and the silicon implant in a ruthless search for perceived perfection.

Keep your answers. Perhaps they've rekindled ambitions, reminded you that there are things you enjoy in life and confirmed that you have talents. Maybe you found out things about yourself that you didn't know, have tried to forget or simply failed to recognise. Or perhaps they have helped you see your way ahead to a different lifestyle, or new career. Remember how good your dream made you feel. Hold on to this sensation and let it inspire you to achieve new goals.

Self-knowledge is vital to becoming confident. You need to recognise your feelings and emotions to learn how to manage them assertively. You need to acknowledge your ambitions and your disappointments in order to make changes. As you go through this book you will add to your store of self-discovery and understanding.

UNDERSTANDING ASSERTION

There is a myth that becoming assertive means turning into superwoman. It's a lie! Superwoman, the one who glides elegantly and effortlessly between immaculate home, impeccably behaved children, a top-flight job, satisfied partner and public position, is more likely to be having a nervous breakdown than swanning around in a designer number baking bread. You cannot do everything, do it well, *and* keep your sanity.

Assertion is about understanding what makes you tick. It means recognising feelings of elation and satisfaction as well as frustration and inadequacy, and learning how to manage them positively. Assertion enables you to take control of your life, to stop looking back and have the confidence to move forward. Assertion is having a deep down, inner belief in yourself.

There's a great deal of confusion about what is and what isn't assertive behaviour. Think about your friends and your colleagues – your boss, your doctor, other professionals you meet. Which of them do you regard as successful and confident? Why? Make a 'confidence hit list'. Consider their personal qualities, the way they behave, how they dress, their voices and mannerisms.

Now consider the following scenario.

> You come home from work one evening. You've had a really rough day. Your head is aching. You walk through your front door to find: your teenage son playing heavy metal at top volume; a pile of dirty plates in the sink and congealed baked beans on the stove top; and a message from your partner saying he's bringing two business associates home for dinner.

How would you react? Would you:

A Storm into the living-room, rip the needle from the heavy metal record and yell at your son, 'You great heaving lout listening to that moronic racket can't you see I've got a headache? You're an ungrateful slob, go and clear up that stinking mess in the kitchen.' Clip him round the ear and walk out. Wrench the receiver off the hook, call your partner and launch into, 'Who do you think I am? I'm not some slave at your beck and call. Go and cook your own lousy dinner.' Slam the phone down.

B Sigh deeply. Walk into the living-room and ask your son (twice) to turn the music down, without success. Sigh. Walk out again. Take some pain-killers. Roll up your sleeves and start the clearing up so that you can get on with the dinner. Say to yourself, 'They're always taking advantage of me. No one cares how I feel. I'm just the family skivvy.' Sigh and frown throughout dinner. When your partner asks you what's the matter you reply, 'Nothing.'

C March into the living-room. Collapse dramatically on the sofa, clutching pain-killers – and your head – and mutter to your son. 'If you don't turn that music off and get into the kitchen to clear up that mess immediately, you can forget going to that party on Saturday – you're grounded.' Silently you vow to drop all his CDs on the floor 'accidentally'. Picking up the telephone, you call your partner: 'By all means bring your associates home but don't expect any favours from me.' Silently you vow to be distinctly uncharming all evening and refuse all his sexual advances for the next month.

As you might have guessed, none of these is an assertive way of dealing with the situation. Why not?

Let's look at response A. This is Aggressive Aggie. She bulldozes her way through life, grinding into the ground everything that comes into her path. She has a habit of bellowing and waving her arms around a lot. Aggressive Aggie takes up a lot of space and people tend to be terrified of her. Because she gets her own way and she's got a loud voice there are those who think she's got confidence. But people don't like being bullied. Although they may agree to Aggressive Aggie's demands, they often harbour resentment and find a way to get back at her later on.

When Aggressive Aggie marched into the living-room and yelled at her son, what might his reaction have been? Well, he would probably have yelled back and an almighty slanging match would have broken out. At the peak of this he would have torn out of the house slamming the door behind him. The result? Two frustrated, fuming individuals, unresolved conflicts about the music and a sink still full of dirty plates. Relations between Aggie and her partner are probably not much better. He gets the message and takes his colleagues to a restaurant, but can you imagine the rows, the sulks and the nasty innuendoes for the next week or so?

Aggressive Aggie lets you know who's boss. The tighter the corner she's in, the more domineering she becomes. Does she really have confidence? No!

What about reaction B? This is Passive Petula, the world's doormat, for everyone walks all over her – and she lets them. Meek and mild, Passive Petula never raises her voice or ventures an opinion. People often ask her to do things for them that they would never dream of asking anyone else to do because they know she won't say no. Passive Petula plays the martyr to seek attention. Her behaviour's so predictable, her friends and acquaintances think she's a bore.

Petula wouldn't dream of confronting her son or her partner over their antisocial habits. She simply moans to herself and plays a sophisticated game of 'guess what's wrong with me'. With enough deep sighing her family get the message and ask. She always replies 'nothing', thereby heightening the drama and the attention she gets – it's so obvious something is wrong. Petula's son and partner know what's going on. They ignore her and go about their own selfish business, knowing she will never challenge them. Passive Petula remains in her dismal rut.

Response C is a bit of a mixture. This is Manipulative Minnie. She displays characteristics similar to both Aggressive Aggie and Passive Petula, but with a style all her own. No one trusts Minnie. She's the sort of person who listens sweetly while you tell her your innermost secrets and then proceeds to broadcast them all over town. She wheels and deals behind people's backs. Quite often Manipulative Minnie gets results and, because she's so nice on the surface, people think she's got confidence. Her 'victims', however, know differently. Like Aggie, she gets caught out in the end.

Manipulative Minnie might succeed in getting her son to turn off the music and clear up. But what about the long term? Minnie can't survive on threats for ever. Her family know the way Minnie works and have developed their own strategies. The plots and counterplots in the household are innumerable and complex. There's never any direct confrontation and the web of truths and half-truths grows more entangled every day.

Now have a look back over your confidence hit list (see page 7). Out of the people you thought had confidence, do any of them behave like Aggressive Aggie or Manipulative Minnie? If you can see some common traits, ask yourself, are these people really confident? Do they truly believe in themselves? Is all the gesturing just a cover up? Do they make you feel good? Or are you the victim of their confidence tricks?

If Aggie represents aggression and both Petula and Minnie represent non-assertive behaviour, what do you have to do to be assertive? Your confidence hit list might give you a clue — providing you haven't crossed off everyone's name!

Let's have a look at how an assertive woman might have handled the same events.

Assertive Woman walks through the door and acknowledges the dirty dishes, the blaring music and the message from her partner. She goes into the living-room, taps her son lightly on the shoulder and says, 'Simon, please turn your music off I want to talk to you ... thank you. I've got a dreadful headache, so I'm not feeling in a particularly good mood. I'm upset that I've come home from work to find your dirty dishes still in the sink and congealed baked beans on the stove. Please go and clear them up immediately, so we can get some supper ready.' Assertive Woman then decides to reply to her partner's message. 'I've just got in and got your message. My head's really thumping and I just don't feel up to entertaining tonight. I imagine you feel a bit let down. Why don't you take them out to a restaurant? Perhaps I can join you later, when I've had a chance to rest.' Assertive Woman recognises that she's dealt with the immediate crises but decides that at a more appropriate time she'll confront her son about helping in the house and her partner about last-minute dinner guests. She'd rather not have to face this scenario again.

Assertive Woman gets results, but this time everyone's ego is still intact, resentments aren't left to fester and the potential long-term problems will be dealt with. This scenario might seem just a little too comfortable for reality, but then we're assuming that an assertive approach is nothing new in this particular household!

Assertive Woman's response highlights some of the key assertion skills: expressing opinions; using positive language; learning to say no; acknowledging other people's feelings; and handling criticism.

Look around you. You often see only very small parts of other people's lives. Take your colleague at work. She might be efficient, sympathetic, an assertive manager, but how does she handle her personal life? What about the woman you see at the school gates, who seems relaxed, in control, at ease with her children. How does she cope in a work situation? The fact is, most of us are assertive in some situations some of the time. Very few people are absolutely assertive in all situations all of the time. What's important is to recognise where and when you feel and act assertively and learn how you can modify your behaviour when you don't.

If everyone behaved assertively, the earth would be an altogether better place. But in the real world people are aggressive and passive and manipulative. Most haven't learnt about how to be assertive, the vast majority don't even know what it is.

Assertion recognises that it takes all sorts to make the world go round and equips you to deal with the human race. You can already recognise the different ways in which people behave and in the following pages you'll find out how to deal with them. You'll understand how to keep your self-respect without undermining theirs, however unpleasant and dogmatic they might be.

If you want to change your life-style and the way you interact with others, remember that your new-found confidence may come as a bit of a shock to the people around you. Take it easy, be patient. They will also need time to adjust. They may not appreciate how you are changing and may try to knock you down. Be gentle, but keep going. Just as you can't become assertive overnight, neither can you expect your nearest and dearest automatically to appreciate the new you — they'll also need time to learn how to adjust.

How assertive are you?

Do you sometimes feel a blind panic when confronting certain situations or overcome with fear when contemplating others? Do you get the wobbles or heart pounding when called upon to perform a particular task or challenge a certain individual?

These exercises are designed to help you find out more about who and what makes you feel uncomfortable and enable you to focus on those situations where you behave less assertively. They'll also enable you to acknowledge those situations which you cope with well.

The 'scoring' for each of the exercises is the same. All you need to do is to mark a number next to each statement.

5 = I never feel comfortable in this situation
4 = I rarely feel comfortable in this situation
3 = I usually feel comfortable in this situation
2 = I almost always feel comfortable in this situation
1 = I always feel comfortable in this situation

Exercise 1 – People

How do you feel when you have to confront the following people? (Confronting can mean asking for information, making a request, giving instructions or criticism and so on: see Chapter 3.)

Younger people 1
Older people 3
Other women 3
Men 5
Family members 3
Professionals (doctors, lawyers, teachers) 4
Technicians (plumbers, carpenters, gardeners, etc) 2
Shopkeepers 2
Aggressive people 3
Passive people 3
People making sexist, sexual or racist comments 3
People you think are more intelligent than you 1
People you think are more attractive than you 3
Someone familiar, one to one 3
A group of people you know well 3
A stranger 3
A group of strangers 3

12

Exercise 2 – **Speaking Up**

How do you feel when you need to speak up in the following situations?

Expressing my opinion 3
Asking for information or clarification 1
Explaining a problem or summing up what has happened 2
Participating in a group discussion 2
Stating my opinion to someone I know will disagree 3
Receiving a compliment about the way I look 4
Complimenting someone else 1
Criticising a colleague for a job done badly 3
Responding to criticism which I think is unfair 2
Responding to criticism which I think is just 1
Saying 'no' to requests for my time 3
Saying 'no' to requests for money 3
Expressing my anger, frustration or disappointment 4
Expressing my happiness, love or desire 1
Making a complaint in a shop or restaurant 2
Socialising at a party 5
Addressing a group of people 4

Exercise 3 – **Issues**

How do you feel when the following subjects come up for discussion?

My achievements 4
My choice of work or career 3
Children and child rearing 3
My family 3
Illness, medical problems and death 3
Money 2
Marriage (including divorce, separation) and life-styles
   generally 2
My personal appearance 2
My past life 3

My mistakes 2
The arts – music, films, books, theatre, TV 1
Food 1
Religion 3
Politics and current social issues 3
Sex 4
Women's equality and rights 3
Prejudice and racial issues 2

Exercise 4 – Specifics

This final exercise is designed to help you focus on those closest to you. It's a very personal list. Please feel free to expand it and make it more specific to suit your own situation. How do you feel about the following?

Partner
Negotiating home responsibilities 1
Discussing/negotiating work issues 1
Discussing/negotiating sex 1

Parents/Family
Handling responsibilities towards other family members 1
Discussing problems of interference 3
Discussing expectations of me 1

Children
Offering praise and encouragement, showing love 1
Discussing problems – work, school, sex, drugs, etc 1
Asking for co-operation 1

Colleagues
Giving criticism 3
Asking for co-operation 1
Handling competition 2

Employers/Clients
    Negotiating workload   3
    Asking for more money or status 2
    Asking for clarification 2

Nanny, cleaner, gardener, other paid help
    Stating what I want done 3
    Discussing money/terms   3
    Handling problems 1

Friends
    Saying no to demands 2
    Stating my own views and opinions 1
    Asking for help 4

Once you've completed the four exercises, you'll begin to build up a clearer picture of the people, situations and issues which you feel comfortable and confident dealing with and those which you don't. To help you do this, mark out three vertical columns on a piece of paper, head the first one '1 & 2', the second '3' and the third '4 & 5'. Fill each column with the situations given in the exercises according to the number you scored against the individual statements.

The longer your list in the column headed '4 & 5' the greater your challenge to become more assertive. Don't despair. Review your list regularly. As you work through this book you should begin shifting those statements up to the number '3' column and then start putting them in the 1s and 2s!

2

Assertive Mind,
Assertive Body

Before you can learn to talk and walk assertively you need to start thinking assertively. In a movie, the actors' minds and bodies become vehicles for the characters they are playing. Their words come from a carefully written script, their delivery and their gestures from a director. Actors don't have to actually *believe* in what they are saying and doing.

In the real world, saying words and carrying out actions just because you know they are assertive isn't enough. Deep down you must believe in what you say and do. Believing in your right to state your view, express opinions, say 'no' to unreasonable requests, is the foundation stone of being assertive.

YOUR RIGHTS CHARTER

These assertion rights are different from what we usually understand as human rights. Human rights might include: the right to a living wage; the right to equal opportunities; the right to education; the right to a roof over your head and so on. Assertion rights are personal rights. They are about your right to take your place in the world and interact with other people. Since these are personal rights, it's up to each individual to come up with her own unique charter of rights.

16

To start you off, here are the golden twelve. They might strike you as very obvious and very ordinary. But do you really believe in them? Sure, you say, what sensible woman wouldn't? When you've read them through once, look at them again and repeat each one out loud. Do you feel comfortable with it, or does it stick in your throat? Are they mere words, or maxims by which you lead your own life?

1 *I have the right to state my own needs and set my own priorities*

Many women spend their lives as someone's daughter or wife or mother or employee – or all four. Are you one of them? Does your day revolve around other people's needs and timetables? Are you the dutiful daughter, the doting mother, the supportive wife, the loyal worker? And if you fulfil all these roles, what do you do for yourself? Who do you tell about your own needs, who do you make demands on?

2 *I have the right to be treated with respect as an intelligent, capable equal*

Sounds good on paper. But what do you do when your car mechanic or your doctor fires off a volley of techno-talk that you're sure is just a lot of waffle? Do you think, 'This doesn't make sense to me, so I must be stupid' or do you ask him to explain it again in plain English?

3 *I have the right to express my feelings*

At least women are not brought up on 'big boys don't cry'. But what do you do when you feel angry or hurt or pleased as punch? Do you set your lips and smile tightly or do you let it all hang out?

4 *I have the right to express my opinions*

What do you do with your views and opinions on the way of the world? Do you keep mum and store them all in a secret internal compartment inside your head, or do you say what you think?

5 *I have the right to say 'yes'*

Do you ever say 'no' when you mean 'yes'? And what happens

when someone questions your decision? Do you stand by it, do you go on the defensive, or do you waiver?

6 *I have the right to say 'no' without feeling guilty*
Do you ever say 'yes' when you mean 'no'? And at what price do you say 'no'; does it leave a nasty imprint on your conscience?

7 *I have the right to lead my life without being dependent on other people's approval*
Why do you do the things you do? Is it because you choose to or because you think someone else would want you to, expect you to or be pleased and proud if you did? How do you deal with disapproval − or do you do your best to avoid it?

8 *I have the right to refuse responsibility for other people's problems*
How much of your day is spent sorting out other people's affairs? Do you deal with their problems at the expense of coping with your own? Do you think you're indispensable?

9 *I have the right to change my mind*
What happens when you agree to do something and then you think your decision may have been a bit hasty? Do you go through with it all regardless or do you call a halt?

10 *I have the right to make mistakes*
Difficult one this. We're taught to do things right and understand the consequences of doing things wrong. Promotion relies on competence. How do you react when you make a mistake? Do you ever stop to consider how small it is?

11 *I have the right to say I don't understand and ask for information*
Own up. When was the last time you said, 'You know I've wondered about that for years but never liked to ask'? The familiar scenario is a group of people leaving a meeting, none of them having understood what was said, none of them daring to ask for an explanation for fear of appearing stupid in front of the others. Was one of them, by any chance, you?

12 *I have the right to make time for myself*
Which brings us back to square one. What do you do for
yourself?

Help yourself to know your rights

1 Make a note next to each of the twelve rights: tick off those
you find easy to say; put a question mark next to those you find
a little difficult and make a cross by those you just can't get your
tongue round.

2 Practise saying each one out loud until you feel at home with
it and it becomes part of your everyday vocabulary. This may
sound like a simple exercise, but don't be surprised or
disillusioned if it takes you time fully to accept some of the
rights.

3 Add to this list other rights which are more specific and more
personal; for example, 'I have the right to say "no" to my son's
requests for money' or 'I have the right to take my holiday when
it's due to me'.

4 Copy out the rights you've come up with and make yourself a
Rights Charter. Keep it by you, like a hip flask, in case of
emergencies!

POSITIVE THINKING

Inside each of our heads is a small voice. It's our staunchest ally
and biggest fan and our cruellest, most vicious critic. It can be
the first to tell us we're the best and pick us up when we are
down. But equally, just when you're feeling warm and good
inside, it often starts nagging, doling out great lashings of
remorse and self-doubt. Who talks most inside your head, ally or
critic?

What does the voice sound like? This might have a familiar

ring: you're standing in front of your wardrobe, getting ready to
go out to a posh do.

> You: *Hm, I think I'll wear the red dress.*
> Small Voice: *The red! That! Why it makes you look
>   positively anaemic. (Bad buy, that.)*
> You: *Okay, not the red. I'll wear the blue suit.*
> Small Voice: *Phew ... bit tarty, don't you think? Bit on
>   the young side. Do you want to look tarty?*
> You: *Er, no. How about the black shirt?*
> Small Voice: *It's all right, but it's got a mark on the
>   front.*
> You: *I can sponge it out.*
> Small Voice: *You can?*
> You: *Yes, look it hardly shows.*
> Small Voice: *Doesn't it? We're going to a smart,
>   sophisticated do, remember?*
> You: *Okay, you're right. How about the pink...?*
> Small Voice: *Now you're talking, that looks smashing...*

This sort of dialogue goes on inside everybody's head, whether
or not we're conscious of it. It's perfectly healthy. It's a
means of letting ourselves stop and think before we open our
mouths or take a decision, it lets us rationalise situations.

Sometimes the small voice bears a remarkable resemblance
to another person − mother or partner or schoolteacher.
Messages you got as a child about your abilities, your looks or
your moral duties, to yourself and others, may still ring in
your head. What matters is whether you harness your small
voice as a powerful tool to help you deal assertively with life
or whether you let it become your dictator.

The critic

Small voices have a habit of using phrases like, 'But you can't do
that', 'you shouldn't', 'you mustn't'. Watch that they don't set
you up to fail. Small voices need challenging.

Martha's on her way to a PTA meeting at her daughter's

school. As she drives along, Martha and her small voice are having this conversation.

Martha: *You know, the idea of the two schools merging is truly appalling. I should say something.*

Small Voice: *You? Say something? You never say anything.*

Martha: *Well, I might.*

Small Voice: *No, you won't. You'll wait until the end when it's too late. You'll probably forget what you were going to say in any case.*

Martha: *And I'll go red and start stammering.*

Small Voice: *Exactly. Remember what happened at the last PTA meeting?*

Martha: *Don't remind me. No, you're right. Anyhow, there's no point everyone getting up and saying the same thing.*

Small Voice: *Exactly. Let the others get on with it.*

Now, let's replay the scene. Supposing Martha started challenging her small voice, the outcome might have been different.

Martha: *You know, the idea of the two schools merging is truly appalling. I should say something.*

Small Voice: *You? Say something? You never say anything.*

Martha: *Well, there's a first time for everything. I've got every right to say what I feel.*

Small Voice: *What right have you got?*

Martha: *Every right. I feel strongly — it's my daughter's school, it's her future, I'm her mother.*

Small Voice: *But you're not an expert.*

Martha: *I'm her mother. She's a pupil. I've the right to put my view.*

Small Voice: *Okay. Go ahead. Make a hash of it.*

Martha: *Why should I make a hash of it?*

Small Voice: *Well you weren't very convincing last time you wanted to say something.*

Martha: *That was last time. I've the right to make mistakes. I know what I want to say this time, I've the right to say it and I'm going to make sure I do.*

Your ally

Sometimes the small voice can be your biggest fan. Your small voice tells you that you *can* do it, you're the best — yet so often you close your ears to it and tell it quite bluntly it's wrong. Start listening to your small voice and accept and trust what it says.

Lara's on her way to a job interview. This is what's going on inside her head.

Lara: *This is going to be dreadful. I don't know why I agreed to go. I'm never going to get the job.*
Small Voice: *Come on, what's up?*
Lara: *I haven't got the right qualifications, I don't know what I'm going to say, I look a mess.*
Small Voice: *Hang on. They wouldn't have invited you for an interview if they didn't think you had the right qualifications, you look fine, your hair really suits you, you do know what to say.*
Lara: *No I don't, I don't.*
Small Voice: *Calm down. Practise your breathing exercise. We went through what you were going to say this morning. You were great. Let's try again ...*

Make an ally of your small voice. Use it to challenge any negative self-image.

Help yourself to positive thinking

1 Think about the small voice inside your head. Does it sound like anyone familiar — a relative or a friend perhaps?

2 Think back over a situation where you've heard your small voice talking inside your head. Make a list of the phrases and messages you've heard it telling you.

22

3 Now consider, are they relevant? Are they fair? Do you like what you hear? Do you believe them? Put a tick next to those comments which you think are positive and a cross by those you think are negative.

4 Go back to the comments marked with a cross. Next to each of them, **write a challenge.** For example:

You shouldn't wear that colour – it's too bright for you.	Why not? I like this colour. It makes me feel good.
Don't go for that job. You won't get it.	How do you know? At least I can have a go. It will be a useful experience – and I could well get it.

FACING UP TO FEELINGS

Emotions are as much a part of us as flesh and blood. You can ignore them, deny them, fight them, but you'll never be free of them. To make assertive choices you need to identify and acknowledge your feelings.

We accept that life's landmarks such as the birth of a baby or the death of a loved one cause people to experience deep emotions, but we tend to ignore the feelings triggered by ordinary, everyday events such as an unexpected compliment from a friend, an argument with a partner, a traffic jam that makes you late for a meeting. We're taught from an early age to hide our emotions. Expressing anger is unladylike, showing fear and crying is weak, leaping for joy is undignified ... and showing affection, well, that's just unBritish.

In learning to hide our feelings from others, we often end up hiding them from ourselves. How often have you denied the way you felt because it seemed illogical, or you thought it was silly, or you felt guilty or ashamed of your feelings? However ridiculous or stupid your feelings seem to you, they are real, even if you don't entirely understand them.

It's important to recognise that feelings change in their intensity according to the situation – and according to the individual. You may feel impatient when you spill a pint of milk, but it's unlikely to be the same degree of anger and frustration you feel when you fail to get a job on the grounds of your sex or colour.

Feelings are physical. Think how your body responds when you're anxious or confused. You probably feel shaky, your heart's pounding, your hands are clammy, you shiver, maybe you feel numb or dizzy. Now consider how your body reacts when you're elated. Do you have an urge to sing and dance, to hug the world? Do you feel sexy, radiant, healthy, like you are walking on air?

The way we breathe, the way we walk, the way we communicate with others are all governed by how we feel. We may not be able to control the feelings we experience, but we can learn to acknowledge them and act on them assertively.

Learning to communicate your feelings assertively is crucial to becoming confident. People express their feelings on three levels. Sometimes you experience a fleeting emotion across your consciousness and think to yourself, 'Hey, that's great' or 'I'm cross about that'. You register it but say or do nothing. On a second level, feelings provoke a verbal reaction. This could be a simple statement such as 'I really feel good about that' or 'I feel very angry'. Finally, feelings find a physical outlet like sobbing or trembling, or hysterical laughter.

In learning to become assertive, you experience new challenges. In these unfamiliar situations you may well find yourself feeling uncomfortable. The most effective way to deal with this is to disclose your feelings. The simple sentence, *'I feel uncomfortable/awkward/embarrassed asking . . .'* will have the immediate effect of reducing your anxiety and putting you back in control. You can then get on with putting your assertive request across.

Next time you're in a sulk or crashing your way around the world, ask yourself: *'What do I feel and why do I feel like this?'* Only then can you begin to make an informed, assertive choice about what to do next.

Help yourself to express your feelings

1 Describe all the sensations you experience when you feel the human race loves and needs you. Your list might include words like: happy, confident, energetic, warm, fulfilled, giving, strong, sexy, outgoing.

2 Now describe all the sensations you experience when you feel unloved and unneeded. This list might include words such as: rejected, shrivelled, cold, miserable, sad, confused, empty, withdrawn, tired.

3 Go back to the exercises on pages 12–15. Select three situations you noted that you have less confidence in. How do you feel when faced with each one?

4 Make a conscious decision to practise using the words '*I feel*...' at least twice each day. And if you're close to someone, don't forget a simple '*I love you*' or '*I care about you*'. That's something worth saying more than once a day!

ASSERTIVE WORDS

If you believe in yourself, you choose what you do with your life. You make the decisions and accept the consequences. You take responsibility for your actions and your words must reflect this.

Non-assertive people don't like taking responsibility for the views and opinions that fall from their lips. They avoid using the word 'I'. Common phrases such as: 'People usually...', 'One likes to believe...' or 'Isn't it...' are not assertive. They are simply an easy way of testing the water. If the crowd disagrees with your viewpoint, you can neatly sidestep any association with what you've just said and go along with the common flow.

If you open your mouth to say something, then own up to the fact that it's your belief or opinion. Don't palm it off as A. N. Other's just because you think someone else might disagree. Try saying: '*I believe*...'; '*I think*...'; '*My view is*...' And only make statements that you know to be true.

Six people walk into a smoke-filled room. You say *'Goodness, it's smoky in here.'* Is that true? Can you guarantee, without discussing it first, that the other five think the room equally smoky? No, you can't. That statement isn't actually true. What's more accurate is the comment, *'Goodness, I think this room's really smoky.'* So next time you're tempted to declare, *'Gosh, it's hot, can we open a window?'* try saying, *'Gosh, I feel hot; I'd like to open a window.'*

How many times in the last week have you used a phrase like, *'I know she'll be really cross...'* or *'I know you're upset...'*? Again, can you guarantee that either of these phrases is true? You've probably got a good idea about how the other person's feeling, but do you know for sure? On the whole, you don't know how other people will react, you can only imagine. Instead of using 'I know' try the words, *'I imagine you feel...'*

Try always to use words that give you choice. *I have to*, *I must*, *I should*, all imply duty. Assertive women make choices. Even if, having thought a situation through, you decide to do something because you feel you have no other option, you have still made a conscious choice. Choice words are: *I want to...*; *I have decided to...*; *I choose to...*

Help yourself to talk assertively

1 Think back over some of the statements you've made in the last twenty-four hours. What words did you use? Were they assertive?

2 Try some of them again, this time using responsible language. Practise beginning sentences with the words, *I think...'* or *'I believe...'* or *'I want to...'*

ASSERTIVE BODY TALK

There can be very few of us who haven't sat in a park or stood at a bus stop and watched the human race go by. As we watch we

26

begin to make judgements about the people we see. We build a picture of who they might be, what they do and where they might be going. Like Sherlock Holmes we watch for clues, the way they walk, the cut of their clothes, their accents, the expressions on their faces. You form an impression of someone you have never met nor exchanged more than a couple of words with. And that impression can be powerful. You may feel warm and drawn towards some people, or perhaps envious of them, or you may take an instant dislike to them. You might think of them as confident or arrogant or weak and non-assertive. What matters is not what they think or say but how they look and how they speak.

The way we walk, our posture and our gestures are a reflection of what we think about ourselves. Consider the way your behaviour changes according to the situation you find yourself in. For example, at an interview you probably sit very tidily, legs together, back straight, taking up very little space. You more than likely feel very tense, conscious that you're not on home ground. Compare that with how you might sprawl comfortably on your sofa at home, relaxed and on your own territory.

If you're tall, and self-conscious about your height, you might try to shrink yourself by stooping. Perhaps you're embarrassed about your skin or your teeth and talk with your hands in front of your mouth. Or maybe you think you're too big – or too flat-chested – and always have your arms across your upper body. The effect of these camouflage techniques is not to draw attention away from our perceived defects but to highlight them. Stooping, putting your hand in front of your mouth and crossing your arms defensively sends out one clear message; 'I don't really feel confident about myself.'

Let's go back to two of the characters we met earlier – Passive Petula and Aggressive Aggie – and imagine what they look like.

Passive Petula does her best not to stand out from the crowd; but she achieves precisely the opposite effect and draws attention to herself. She doesn't walk, she shuffles, shoulders hunched up to her ears, head down. When she meets someone, her arm slides out to suggest the merest hint of a greeting. On rare occasions she proffers a limp hand. Her eyes remain firmly fixed on her acquaintance's boots. When she talks, Passive Petula shifts her hand nervously in front of her mouth, causing a chorus of, 'I'm sorry, could you repeat that?' Oh, and Passive Petula twiddles her hair. It's something she began at the tender age of two and has failed to grow out of.

Aggressive Aggie, on the other hand, wants to make her presence felt. She strides about the place like a tornado in a hurry, head flung back, arms akimbo. When she sits down she spreads herself and her belongings across two places. Since she has a habit of bellowing, no one likes sitting too close in any case. It's very strange but if you watch Aggressive Aggie at any social gathering, you'll see her moving slowly across the floor as her conversation partner tries desperately to back away from her clutches.

There really isn't any mystique about assertive body language. It's simply a matter of making sure that your gestures and your appearance are appropriate to the situation and match the words you use. Remember, confidence comes from within. The more you begin to think assertively and find assertive solutions to everyday situations, the easier it will become to look assertive.

How can you make a more confident impression?

Walk tall, sit straight. We can't all move with the grace and ease of a trained dancer, but it's a goal worth aiming for. Look at yourself in the mirror. Stand sideways. Is your body in a don't care, couch potato shape? Are your shoulders and stomach in a free fall slouch? Do you look as if the burdens of the world have fallen heavily on your shoulders? Well maybe things aren't that bad, but if you're not radiating catwalk confidence, perhaps a little fine tuning wouldn't go amiss.

For a start, stand up straight. That doesn't mean you fling yur bust skywards and take in one enormous breath in an attempt to get your tummy flat. Try this instead.

1 Relax your shoulders. Hunch them up to your ears, then slowly rotate them backwards and as you do so relax them downwards.

2 Pull in your tummy muscles and tilt your pelvis forwards slightly in the cowboy style of John Wayne. Pulling in your stomach and thrusting out your bottom like a sergeant major, will only give you severe back ache.

3 Stretch your neck by lifting your chin towards the ceiling, then let your head align itself naturally with the rest of your body.

Your spine should now be set straight. There should be no exaggerated curve and the position should feel comfortable.

Loosen up your arms. Get used to the sensation of swinging them by your side. Don't swing them too high − you don't want to look like a drum majorette on parade. But neither do you want to look like a stiff wooden doll.

Now try walking across the room. Pick out something at eye level at the opposite end of the room and walk towards it without looking at the ground. If all else fails, try the old finishing school trick − balance a book on your head.

When you sit down, try to push the base of your spine into the back of the chair. Put both your feet firmly on the ground. This has nothing to do with ladylike postures, it simply makes good back-care sense. Remember to keep your shoulders back and in a relaxed position.

To free your body up, consider taking up a dance or aerobics class or learning the Alexander Techniques or T'ai Chi.

Eye contact is probably one of the most powerful forms of nonverbal communication. Ignore it at your peril. Eyes reflect the mood, the desires, the anxieties and the attentiveness of both speaker and listener. Avoiding eye contact is like having a conversation on the telephone, you can never truly judge whether the other person is paying attention to what you have to say and you often haven't a clue about what they are really feeling. Imagine talking face to face to someone who's wearing reflective sunglasses. It can be a pretty unnerving experience and the effect is much the same as avoiding eye contact.

Making eye contact does not mean staring fixedly into someone's eyeballs. A fixed stare can make the other person feel uncomfortable − even threatened. On the other hand, glancing up or down or from side to side, when you meet someone, gives the impression that you feel uneasy, or that you're shifty and not to be trusted, or that you're simply not interested in them.

Instead of homing-in on someone's eyes, try to take in the total face – forehead, nose, cheeks, mouth, hair. If you alternate between each feature, including the eyes, you will give the impression of making effective eye contact without falling into the trap of staring.

Whether you're doing the talking or listening keep your eyes in contact, they're a very powerful ally. For more about listening skills turn to page 60.

Find your distance. Have you ever found yourself edging away from someone just to get the face back in focus? What about joining a group at a party? Do you sidle up or barge straight in?

We all respond to an invisible line between ourselves and others on which we feel comfortable and effective. Too far over the line and we feel we're breathing down someone's neck. Too far away and it's hard to attract the other person's attention. The point is, each of us draws this personal comfort line at a different distance. Consequently, when we meet someone, we often have to renegotiate it. Some people abuse the comfort line to make others feel uneasy. They may keep their distance, so that you find it extremely difficult to strike up any kind of rapport or converse without raising your voice inappropriately. Other people, and men are usually the biggest culprits, have a habit of invading personal space. The worst examples of this are the arm-draping, knee-brushing brigade. Many women find such behaviour unnecessary and intimidating. Use your assertion skills to re-establish your own comfort line. Remember, though, that each country and culture will have its own acceptable comfort line. Be aware of this – and be prepared to compromise!

Don't let others use height or distance to take advantage of you.

Charlene used to find it difficult to approach her boss. He had a huge office and sat behind an enormous desk. Charlene found that she tended to hover around the door and her boss would ignore her or tell her to come back later. Now when Charlene goes to see her boss, she knocks sharply at the door and, when told to enter, walks assertively up to her boss's desk before she makes her request. Her boss finds it much harder to dismiss her presence.

In the same way, watch that you don't find yourself making an all important request whilst craning your neck back at your boss who's towering over you.

Zoe wanted to ask for a pay rise. She made an appointment to see her manager and he asked her to take a seat. As she began to make her request for more money, her boss got up and came to stand beside her chair. Zoe felt she couldn't negotiate assertively from her lowly position and stood up as well. Her boss returned to his seat but Zoe felt more confident standing and remained where she was.

If you feel more comfortable standing in this sort of situation and someone presses you to take a seat, try saying, '*Thank you, but I'd prefer to stand for the moment.*' Sit down when you feel it's appropriate.

When you talk to someone, try to face them square on. This can be quite difficult to do when you find yourself in a group. If you're in this situation, try to turn squarely towards the person or people you're addressing; this might mean blocking out someone else in the group for a moment, but you should find the others attend to what you are saying.

However assertive your message, if you can't put it over, it becomes worthless. Make sure you're in a position to come across with confidence.

Get a grip. People carry out quite incredible feats with their arms and hands, especially when they're standing still. What do you do with yours?

Gestures are a vital part of nonverbal communication, adding colour to social interaction. The important thing is to make sure your gestures are appropriate. Hair twiddling, scalp scratching, pulling at clothes, biting at fingers and mouth, clasping and unclasping hands are all signs of nervousness and tension. Foot

31

and finger tapping send out messages of impatience. Sharp, chopping movements signal anger.

If you don't know what to do with your hands and you can't place a drink or a vol-au-vent in them, then try putting them behind your back or hanging loosely by your sides. To help yourself relax, place the back of one hand against the palm of the other in a gently cupped position. This is very useful if you're sitting down. It's virtually impossible to twist your fingers into a nervous knot in this position. By all means use your hands to make a point, but don't wave them around so that you look like a windmill.

Handshakes are a social necessity. They're often a vital part of the first − and the last − impression we make when we meet someone. What sort of hand do you offer − limp and delicate, clammy, knuckle cracking? Don't be afraid to put your hand out first; be purposeful. Clasp the other person's hand warmly and firmly and hold the handshake for three or four seconds. Make eye contact as you grasp his or her hand. Smile!

You can practise this with a telephone receiver! The old-fashioned, curved ones work best. Hold the receiver in your left hand, put your right arm out, grasp the receiver as you would a hand and give it a firm handshake. Smile, and say, *'I'm delighted to meet you!'*

Making assertive sounds

It's not what you say, it's the way that you say it. This isn't just about standing up straight and not shuffling, it's about the expression on your face and the way you use your voice. Do you sound what you mean?

Claire is a manager in a department store. She's good at her job but finds difficulty asserting her authority over junior staff. When she had to confront a young salesgirl about her rudeness to a customer and her general attitude to work, Claire told the girl that she was giving her a verbal warning and that if her attitude didn't improve she would be out of a job. The problem was not what Claire actually said, but the way she said it. She carried out the entire disciplinary interview with a smile on her face and ended each sentence with a nervous giggle. No wonder the girl commented that she didn't believe Claire would carry out her warning.

If you feel angry about something and begin your sentence, *'I'm extremely cross about. . . '* then there's no point in continuing if you have a huge grin on your face. Make sure your facial expression complements, not contradicts, the words that come out of your mouth.

The tone, volume and inflections of your voice also make a difference to the meaning of your sentences. Try this exercise. Repeat the following sentence six times. Each time emphasise a different word and you'll see how the meaning of the sentence can change completely.

*'**Would** you like to go to this party?'*
If I were to invite you, would you want to go?

*'Would **you** like to go to this party?'*
Would you, rather than anyone else, like to go?'

*'Would you **like** to go to this party?*
Does the idea really appeal?

*'Would you like **to go** to this party?'*
Do you actually want to go along?

*'Would you like to go to **this** party?'*
This party, as opposed to another one.

*'Would you like to go to this **party**?*
Some party, uh?!

Now try the sentence using voices that reflect different kinds of moods. Try saying it very angrily; jokingly; accusingly; sadly. Watch yourself in a mirror as you repeat the sentence and see how your facial expressions change according to the feeling you're trying to convey.

How you use your voice can also make all the difference between making a firm assertive statement and turning it into a quivering question. If you raise your voice at the end of a sentence you automatically turn it into a question. Questions invite responses and you may well not want one. Try the following request twice. Read it once keeping your voice firmly down at the end and a second time raising it on the last word.

This spaghetti is inedible. Please will you get the manager.

By keeping your voice on much the same level you make the statement, *'Please go and get the manager, I want to see him now'*. By raising your voice at the end, you turn the same request into, *'Is it at all possible to see the manager?'* No prizes for guessing which approach is more likely to get results. If you're sure about what you want to say, make sure you make a statement and don't ask a question that begs an answer.

Finally, a word about volume. Whispering and mumbling should be kept strictly for lovers' ears and party games. Like everything else to do with assertion, the way you deliver your message must be clear and unambiguous. Don't restrict the volume of your voice by covering up your mouth or talking down at your shoes. If other people keep asking you to speak up or repeat what you've said, then maybe you're not speaking clearly and loudly enough. The more confident you become about what you have to say, the less of a hurdle you'll find it to project your voice more loudly.

Help yourself to assertive body talk

1 Find out more about your personal body language. Ask a trusted friend to tell you about any obvious or irritating habits. If you get the chance, watch yourself on a video — you might get some surprises!

2 Try standing and sitting positions using very negative body language — arms crossed, hunched up, legs twisted, eyes down, fidgeting, hand in front of mouth. Imagine you are having a conversation with someone. Watch yourself in a mirror. Now try those positions again using positive body language. Make a mental note of the different effects.

3 Make a list of specific gestures or examples of body language you want to change. Fix an image of those negative habits in your mind and use them to challenge yourself when you're out and about.

4 Practise using your voice in different ways. Take a short recipe and read it out loud using the different moods suggested in the exercise on page 33.

5 Also try alternately whispering the ingredients and then saying them very loudly. This is especially useful if you usually speak quietly; you'll be able to recognise the difference in the level of your voice and begin to find an acceptable medium.

6 Stand in front of a mirror and repeat the following sentences. Watch carefully to make sure your mouth and eyes change depending on which sentence you are saying.

> *I feel really happy.*
> *I'm absolutely furious.*
> *I'm so pleased to meet you, I've heard such a lot about you.*
> *I feel very hurt by what you just said.*

7 Try joining a drama, play-reading or public speaking group at your local adult education college.

Exercises to calm nerves

When you're confronted with a situation which causes you anxiety, you may find yourself starting to feel slightly light-headed or short of breath, and your heart might start beating faster. This is because anxiety causes us to take in shallower breaths and not breathe out as frequently as we normally do. A simple breathing relaxation exercise can help you to calm down and regain control of the situation.

If you feel yourself getting worked up or angry, or you're tense, practise this easy calming trick.

The three-second calmer

1 Breathe in deeply through your mouth.

2 Hold it for three seconds

3 Blow out all the air until you have none left – keep pushing until it's all gone.

4 Don't breathe for three seconds.

5 Repeat steps 1, 2, 3, 4, twice more.

6 The third time you do the exercise, continue to breathe normally.

You may feel a little light-headed but it'll soon pass.

This second exercise is useful if you're feeling nervous just before making a presentation, or you're called on to speak to a meeting, or you're about to go into an interview. Practise these few moves before you leave your seat:

The pre-presentation relaxer

1 Breathe in slowly through your mouth.

2 As you do so hunch your shoulders up tight under your ears, hold for a second.

3 Then slowly relax your shoulders as you breathe out.

4 Sit back straight in your chair, feet firmly on the ground.

5 Cup the back of one hand in the palm of the other and relax your fingers.

6 Think to yourself, 'I'm going to be great!'

3

Assertion Essentials

Whatever your life-style, interacting with other human beings is all part of the daily routine. In this chapter we'll be looking at techniques for handling basic encounters assertively, including how to say 'no' and how to manage feelings of anger. The last part of this chapter shows you how to write a 'survival script' to help you prepare for the trickiest confrontations.

MAKING REQUESTS

What happens when you want someone to do something? Do you hint subtly or do you ask outright? If you find yourself making comments like, '*You know, I'm always telling her...*', perhaps you've not been speaking plainly. Learning to make clear and direct requests is vital to becoming assertive.

There are three simple steps to making assertive requests:

1 Decide what it is you feel or want.

2 Say so. Be direct. Be specific.

3 Stick to it. Don't get led astray. Repeat your request.

Once you've decided what it is you want or feel, you need to formulate one or two sentences that express your needs or emotions. What you say must be specific and expressed directly. When you've worked out what to say — stick to it. Don't hedge around the subject and hope it'll go away.

Avoid padding out your sentences:
'I'm terribly sorry to bother you, I hate to be a nuisance, but would you mind, *I'd like you to change this for a clean knife.*'
'I wondered, if by any chance, um, you might, um, look, don't bother if you aren't free, but *could you please baby-sit for me this afternoon?*'
These are not assertive ways to make a request or to respond to a request. Go straight in. You're not being blunt, you're being honest and direct. If you beat around the bush, you may end up sending out very confusing messages.

You need to state clearly what the issue is and what you want done about it. Again, your aim is to be unambiguous. Let's suppose you bought an expensive leather bag in your local boutique and a week later it fell apart. You feel very cross and decide you want your money back. Think through what you're going to say and come up with a basic request:
'*I bought this bag from you last week. I have used it once and the strap has broken. Please can I have my money back.*'
(Remember to keep that last sentence a statement; don't raise your voice at the end and turn it into a question.)

Now you've stated your basic request you need to stick by it and not get led astray. If the other person responds positively and respects your request without question, then you're home and dry. But what if they don't? You need to think about the sort of responses you might get and how you would deal with them. Your aim is to acknowledge the response but stick hard and fast to your original request.

There are three sorts of responses you might get:

The Irrelevant Response is the one many people fall for without realising it and are halfway up the garden path and through the gate before it dawns on them. The respondent replies with a statement which, if you think about it, has absolutely nothing to do with the outcome of your request. For example, the shop assistant might say: *'Oh, that's nothing to do with me, I wasn't here last week.'* Your assertive response to this would be: *'I bought this bag in this shop last week, here's my receipt. The strap's broken and I want my money back.'*

The Argumentative Response is the one that fuels the start of World War Three. Have you ever ended up having had a whirlwind of a row and then thought to yourself, 'But I only asked if...'? Learn to recognise responses that are trying to manipulate you into an argument. If you fall for it, you will weaken your case. Let's follow the bag with the broken strap example one step further; the sales assistant: *'Well, obviously, if you buy a bag like this you should learn to take care of it. If you want a bag to throw around, you shouldn't shop here.'*

Your assertive reply to this argumentative response might be: *'I know how to look after expensive leather bags. This one is broken and I want my money back.'*

There's more about avoiding and handling arguments on pages 49–52, under Dealing with Confrontation.

The Guilt Trip Response aims to make you feel thoroughly ashamed of what you've just said. Women are particularly easy prey for the wily guilt tripper. We'll look more at dealing with feelings of guilt in the next section, Saying 'No'.

Following on with the broken bag example, how might the guilt trip response be played? The sales assistant could say: *'Look, I'm sorry, you can see we're terribly busy and you're holding everyone else up. If you'd just let them all through.'* Your assertive response might be: *'I can see that you're terribly busy, but I bought this bag from your shop last week, the strap's broken and I want my money back.'*

Sticking to your request and repeating your original statement is known as the 'broken record' technique — saying the same thing over and over again. To communicate effectively you must ensure that you acknowledge what the other person has said before reiterating your request.

Let's have a look at how you might reply to irrelevant and guilt trip responses in other situations:

'I can see no one else in the restaurant is complaining, but this steak is inedible and I'd like another one.'

'I understand that no one else has ever returned a toaster to you, but this one is faulty and I'd like my money back.'

'I'm sure your children won't be a bother, but I'm still not prepared to look after them this afternoon.'

'I appreciate everything you've done for me in the past, but I'm unable to do your shopping this afternoon.'

'I know you're tired too, but I need you to help me do this.'

'I imagine you do feel let down, but I still don't want to go away this weekend.'

For more about how and when to make requests see pages 49–52, Dealing With Confrontation.

Help yourself to make requests

Practise making requests. There's no substitute for doing the real thing, but it helps to rehearse, either with a friend or trusted ally or by yourself. Imagine how you would approach the following situations:

- Asking a friend to return a valuable book borrowed six months ago.
- Asking a waitress in a café to bring you another cake as the one you have is stale.
- Taking a faulty radio back to a shop.

SAYING 'NO'

Many women have great problems with the word 'no'. Although, thankfully, attitudes are changing, most little girls are still taught to be sweet and compliant and to acquiesce to every request. Only naughty, ungrateful, thoughtless girls say 'no'. And when we get older, the word 'no' takes on new meanings, especially in a sexual context. According to popular belief, when a woman says 'no' she actually means 'yes'. Assertion is about saying 'no' when you mean no and 'yes' when you mean yes. That's all very well but watch that your noes and your yeses don't get caught up in a nasty web of pity, guilt and innuendo.

Let's explode some of these myths about 'no':

Saying 'no' is mean, uncaring and selfish.
Saying 'no' is petty and small-minded.
Saying 'no' directly is blunt and rude.
Saying 'no' will only make others feel hurt and rejected.

Is it assertive to feel you have to put someone else's needs before your own? Is it assertive to let someone else decide what is and is not important to you? Is it assertive to give ambiguous, indirect messages about what you want and how you feel? Is it assertive to avoid hurting someone else's feelings at all costs?

The answer to all these questions is a resounding 'no'! If you found yourself answering 'yes', then look back to Your Rights Charter, pages 16–19.

What happens when you agree to do something you really don't want to do? How many seconds after you've said 'yes' do you start planning how to avoid the request? Even when our lips say 'yes' our bodies start saying 'no'. That sinking feeling in the pit of your stomach, the tensing of your facial muscles and your forced smile are more reliable indicators of whether or not what you really want to say is 'no'. If your body is telling you to say 'no', then make sure your lips follow suit.

What is the end result of saying 'yes' when what you really meant was 'no'? Come the day of the party, function, jumble sale or whatever, you wake up suddenly not feeling too good. A throbbing headache or unsettled stomach threatens and you feel more than justified in calling to give your apologies. Miraculously, you feel ten times better as soon as you put the phone down. This is the fake 'yes'. And if you're honest you've been working on saying 'no' since you first said 'yes'.

Saying 'no' is not selfish or mean or rude. Saying 'no' when you mean 'no' is assertive. So how do you do it?

The golden rule to remember is, *when you say 'no', you reject the request not the person*. Try saying that over to yourself until you feel comfortable with it. You are not telling the person you don't want them, love them or respect them, merely that you're not prepared to carry out what they've asked you to do.

Gloria telephones her mother to say that she won't be able to visit her on her birthday.

Gloria: *Hi, Mum, how are you?*

Mum: *Oh, Gloria, I'm glad you called, I was just making arrangements for my birthday. When are you arriving?*

Gloria: *Yes, that's why I called. I'm sorry but I won't be able to come up until the following Saturday. I've got something on at work.*

Mum: *Oh Gloria, that's dreadful. I was so looking forward to your visit. Please change your mind and come up on my birthday.*

Gloria: *No, Mum, I've decided I want to stay here for this project at work. I can hear you're disappointed, but I'll be up the following weekend. I want us to do something really special. Tell me where you'd like to go.*

Here are some more techniques to help you handle saying 'no'.

Buy yourself time. When you're put on the spot and asked for a snap decision you might find yourself more inclined to say 'yes'. Don't be hurried into making a response you'll regret. Try one of the following phrases:

'I need some more information before I can give you an answer.'
'Sounds interesting, but I want some time to think it over.'
'I can't give you an answer immediately.'
'Thanks for asking me ... let me come back to you.'
'I'd like to check first in my diary ... talk it over with...'

Be direct. Don't hedge around in the vain hope the other person will get the message. Avoid saying things like, 'Look, I'm really sorry... under normal circumstances... I hope you won't think I'm mean...' Don't pad out your 'no' with excessive apologies. Go straight in:

I'm sorry I can't help you...
I'm not prepared to...
No, not today...

Don't hang around. Once you've said 'no', and it's been accepted, move on. Witness this exchange in how *not* to reject a request.

Kate: *I don't want to go out tonight, I'm incredibly tired. Perhaps another night.*
Jack: *Fine, no problem, maybe next Saturday.*
Kate: *Look I hope you're not upset or anything. I feel really mean...*
Jack: *No it's okay, another night will be great.*
Kate: *Are you sure... etc, etc.*

If only Kate had accepted Jack's response.

Kate: *I don't want to go out tonight, I'm incredibly tired. Perhaps another night.*
Jack: *Fine, no problem, maybe next Saturday.*
Kate: *Great, that would be fun. What time?*

Remember to use assertive language and to acknowledge your feelings and those of the other person.

Next time you're in the least bit tempted to say 'yes' when you mean 'no', consider how you felt when someone rang you at the last moment, with an unconvincing excuse, to cancel an engagement. Bet you said something to the effect of, 'Why on earth didn't she just say no in the beginning!'

Help yourself to say 'no'

1 Practise saying the word 'no'.

2 Think of three requests that have come up recently: one which you were more than happy to accept; one which you wanted to say 'no' to but said 'yes' to instead; and one which you had no problem in saying 'no' to. Repeat each of your responses in front of a mirror and see how your facial expressions change. How comfortable did you feel with each response?

3 Practise a new 'no' response to the situation which you originally non-assertively agreed to. Consider how you feel after saying 'no' and how you felt previously when you replied 'yes'.

4 Next time you're asked to do something, check your reactions – is your body saying 'yes' or 'no'? – and act on them.

BEING ANGRY

How do you react when you feel angry? Do you bite your lip and keep quiet? Perhaps you simply walk away from the situation. Or do you let your anger simmer for days and then blow up? Who feels the brunt of your anger – is it usually someone or something other than the person you're actually angry with? Experiencing and expressing anger is part of being assertive. Learn to recognise and manage those feelings.

Let's return to the characters we met at the beginning of the book – Aggressive Aggie, Passive Petula and Manipulative Minnie. How do they handle anger?

Aggressive Aggie, as you might imagine, lashes out. The tiniest spark turns her into a fireball, spitting and hitting. Her violent outbursts are aimed at whoever happens to be in her line of fire at the time. She never stops to consider the extent of her anger; whatever the cause, the treatment meted out is much the same.

Passive Petula doesn't express anger. She sometimes cries when she feels frustrated and cross and everyone thinks she is upset. Or she smiles – and everyone thinks all is okay. Passive Petula's anger gnaws away inside her. On the occasions she suddenly lets it all out, she is instantly overcome with remorse and guilt.

Manipulative Minnie carries her anger around with her like Passive Petula. But she also has a tendency to spit and hit. Only this time, it's not like Aggressive Aggie's great fireball, Minnie's barbs are carefully aimed. Like poisoned darts they make their mark — the cutting comment, the look that says, 'Wait until I get my own back on you.'

Over the years we get all sorts of messages about how we should deal with anger: 'You're not a pretty sight when you scowl'; 'Stop getting so hysterical, you sound like a fishwife'; 'Count to ten before you say anything'. Is it any wonder, then, that we don't know what to do with the powerful emotions we experience? The first step to dealing assertively with anger is to recognise what anger is and what causes it.

The root cause of anger is often unmet expectations. We become frustrated because we can't do something we wanted to, or have tried and failed to achieve some goal. We feel angry and let down because someone or something did not live up to our expectations. But why do some situations cause us to react with a great deal of anger and others not?

What's the threat? When we're faced with a situation that feels unfamiliar or uncomfortable, we attempt to analyse it. How threatening is it? Will we come out on top? If we feel powerful, the threat goes away and maybe we're just left with a sensation of annoyance. If we perceive the threat as one which makes us powerless, we may feel anger. Take this simple example:

On Monday morning Jan is on her way into work, driving along towards the main road where there's just been an accident. She sees a long queue of traffic ahead. Her immediate thought is that she'll be late for work, but then she realises that she doesn't have any urgent appointments. As she hasn't yet got on to the main road she decides to take another route. This delays her slightly. She's mildly annoyed by the whole episode.

The following Monday, Jan's in a tearing hurry. She's due in her office early for an important meeting. As she gets to the main road, she finds herself in the middle of a slow moving contra-flow system. Jan thinks to herself, this is going to hold me up, I'm going to be late and there's nothing I can do about it. She starts swearing and hitting the steering wheel.

On the face of it, you have two similar situations but two very different reactions. On the first occasion Jan realises that there's no major threat to her. It doesn't matter whether she's late for work and in any case she finds an alternative route. In the second, Jan perceives not only that she has no control over the route she's taking but that she has a lot to lose if she's late.

Use your body as a barometer to help you recognise feelings of anger. You may sense yourself tensing – clenching your hands and your jaw, your heart might start pounding, you may feel like bursting into tears. Having begun to recognise anger and understand what it is about, how can you handle it assertively?

To deal assertively with anger, you have to get your feelings into perspective. Ask yourself, 'How big is the threat?', 'How angry am I?', 'How important is this situation?' Imagine an anger ladder that goes something like this:

going to blow a fuse!

furious

incensed

indignant

annoyed

impatient

Displeased

The anger ladder is here to help you get your feelings into perspective. It allows you room to manoeuvre. Before you jump off the deep end and threaten someone with full-blooded murder, think about how far you might have to climb to get what

46

you want. Are you really about to blow a fuse or are you simply impatient with the situation? Don't leave yourself with no more rungs to climb.

Imagine you have a nine-year-old son who won't go to bed at night and sits up playing computer games for hours on end. You feel pretty frustrated by the situation. How might an anger ladder be put into practice?

Rung One: *Billy, I'm getting impatient – you're still up. Turn the light off and get into bed.* (Billy gets the benefit of the doubt.)

Rung Two: (Louder and firmer voice) *Billy, I'm cross. Turn the light off immediately and get into bed.*

Rung Three: (Going into room) *Billy, I'm very angry that you're not in bed. Turn that light off now, or I'm taking the computer away.*

Rung Four means you have to deal with taking the computer away. Don't issue threats that you have no intention of carrying out; they're worthless.

Communicate your feeling of anger

In Chapter 2 we looked at the importance of acknowledging and expressing feelings. Keeping your emotions in check, to the extent that what you say and the way that you say it is appropriate to the situation, can be especially difficult when you're angry. The key to being able to communicate effectively without becoming sarcastic or overbearing is to try to relax. When you're angry, you become anxious. This in turn restricts your breathing. As a result your throat tightens and you end up sounding panicky. To find out more about how to relax turn to page 35.

A simple statement, such as 'I'm cross' or 'I'm angry', if said assertively, at the right speed and volume, can be an effective way of putting your message across. Make sure that the tone of your voice and your facial expressions match what you are saying.

It's all right to let off steam. A good cry or scream can release all your inner tensions and frustrations. Scrubbing the floor, pummelling a cushion, kneading bread, slamming doors, stamping hard, all work equally well. It's not so much what you do, but when and where you do it. Bursting into floods of tears or hurling abuse at your boss are not particularly sensible ways to release pent-up frustration at a business meeting. A deep breathing exercise in the privacy of the loo or a short walk round the block may provide a more appropriate means to help you feel calmer and better able to deal assertively with the situation.

However you choose to let off steam, watch that it's right for the moment. Hit the wall or the sofa, not your kids. Rather kick the door than the dog.

How do you react when someone else directs their anger towards you? Many people feel terrified when faced by another person in a fit of temper. To interrupt a torrent of angry abuse or hysterical behaviour you first need to grab the other person's attention. To do this, repeat a single word or a short phrase such as '*Stop that!*' or '*Listen to me*" or else say the person's name, over and over again. You'll need to make sure that your voice is firm and strong and can be heard by the other person. It may be appropriate, particularly where the other person is a child or someone close to you, to put an arm round them and cuddle them gently. Obviously don't try and do this if they're hitting out physically.

Try to catch the other person's eye – the sound of your voice will probably make them look at you. As soon as you make eye contact, say something like: '*I can see you're angry, when you calm down we'll talk*' or '*I know you're angry, but when you're like this I'm frightened.*'

If you can't or don't want to confront the person, then don't feel compelled to stay. Walk away until they have calmed down.

Help yourself to deal with anger

1 Make a list of all the things that make you feel angry – your list might include events, people, habits, things that irritate and those that infuriate.

2 Next to each item you've listed write down how you react to each one.

3 Think about the last time you got really angry. How did you react? If you had to deal with the situation again, how do you think you might handle it second time round?

4 Make a list of all the ways that you let off steam, where and when you do it. Consider whether or not they are appropriate to the situation.

5 Practise the relaxation exercises on page 36.

DEALING WITH CONFRONTATION

The word 'confrontation' is often used today to convey an image of aggression and hostility. Most day-to-day confrontations are straightforward requests for, or exchanges of, views and information, like making a purchase or asking a child how she got on at school. Because they are achieved easily, we tend not to see these sorts of situations as confrontations.

When the stakes are raised, then the request or exchange of information takes on a new perspective, for example if you need to see your boss about a major project or you have to return a faulty item to a shop. We start talking about 'confronting so and so about...' Don't avoid or be afraid of confrontation. Remember that the word simply means a face-to-face meeting, so don't go looking for, or expecting a fight.

Do you ever find yourself mentally battered after a major slanging match wondering how on earth you both got into such hot water? Everyday life is littered with potential war zones, just waiting for us to trip into them. Tame meetings become battles of will — one misunderstood remark, and the superpowers have their fingers on the red button. How easily we see simple interactions as potential attacks and how quickly they become major conflagrations. Learn to recognise a battlefield and understand how to disarm any warring factions.

Let's look at a potentially explosive situation and see how it can be deflected.

> Judy: *Bob, look what you've done, you've splashed dirty water all over my paperwork. I told you not to clean your filthy bike in here.*
>
> Bob: *Oh, sorry, I didn't notice you were working.*
>
> Judy: *Didn't notice? You just don't care. Look it's ruined. You're so selfish. If I'd touched your precious bike...*
>
> Bob: *Oh shut up, it's not ruined, stop making a drama.*
>
> Judy: *Oh, and look who's talking. You like the money I bring in but you never stop complaining when I bring work home. I just can't please you, can I?*
>
> Bob: *No you can't. If you spent more time thinking about me and the kids and less about that blooming job of yours...*
>
> Judy: *Don't you dare start that again, you're not exactly Mr Perfect... etc, etc.*

And so a conversation about splashed water escalates into a substantial and destructive set-to.

Now let's replay it, with Bob acting assertively, acutely aware that Judy is raring to start a fight.

> Judy: *Bob, look what you've done, you've splashed dirty water all over my paperwork. I told you not to clean your filthy bike in here.*
>
> Bob: *Oh, sorry, I didn't notice you were working.*
>
> Judy: *Didn't notice? You just don't care. Look it's ruined. You're so selfish. If I'd touched your precious bike...*
>
> Bob: *Judy, I really am sorry. I didn't think...*
>
> Judy: *I just don't believe you, you don't care...*
>
> Bob: *I said I was sorry. Look I'll clear up this minute. Let's see if we can do something with that piece of paper.*

Practise using the 'broken record' technique described on pages

37–40. Also listen to your body to detect signs of anger. If you find yourself being drawn unwittingly on to a battlefield, retreat. Use a phrase such as:

'Look, this isn't getting us anywhere, let's talk again later.'
'There's no point discussing this further until we both calm down.'
'I'm not prepared to get drawn into an argument, let's drop the subject.'

Successful confrontations depend not only on the words you use to handle the situation but also on the time and place.

Don't expect to have a sensible, productive discussion with your teenage son, when he returns home full of good spirits and somewhat on the defensive at two o'clock in the morning. Equally, it's not a particularly good idea to start talking to your partner about the meaning of life and the future of your relationship in bed, when you're both exhausted. And if you need to see your boss or a work colleague about an important matter, you don't want to attempt it while the phone is ringing every two minutes and other people come flying in and out of the office.

Make sure you give yourself the time and space to say what you want to say. Get on the 'right side' of the other person – don't make them feel uncomfortable, ensure that you have their full attention. You might want to try using phrases such as:

'I feel very upset/angry about . . . I don't think it's appropriate to discuss it now, so let's make a time to talk about it on. . .'

'I can see you're tied up/watching TV/doing your homework, but I want to talk to you when you're finished.'

'I'd like to talk to you in private. Could we arrange a time (half an hour, an hour. . .) to meet when you'll be free from interruptions?'

'I can see you're busy; when will you be free?'

If you find yourself in the middle of a discussion which is proving fruitless, perhaps because the phone is constantly ringing, other people keep interfering or the person you are talking to is obviously preoccupied, then stop the conversation if you can. You could try saying something like:

'Look, I really don't feel comfortable discussing this with so

many people around, I'd prefer it if we could go somewhere quieter' or *'You seem to be very preoccupied/tired, perhaps we can talk about this tomorrow.'*

Make life easier for yourself. Get the time and the place right if you have to confront a difficult situation.

Help yourself to manage confrontation

1 Consider the last time you got into an argument with someone. Why do you think it happened? What could you have done that would have changed the outcome?

2 Next time you have to confront a difficult situation, think long and hard about where and how you could approach it. Also have a look at How to Write a Survival Script, pages 63 – 66.

TAKING AND GIVING CRITICISM

How do you react to the word criticism? Does it leave a nasty tight sensation in the pit of your stomach? As children we are bombarded with criticism from parents, teachers and peers. Kids get labelled 'stupid' or 'clumsy', teased for being slow at games or having spots. Degraded and humiliated, we learn to associate criticism with a sense of rejection. Is it any wonder that by adulthood we don't know how to give or accept it?

Criticism can be good or bad. Even when it involves confronting someone over shoddy work or a poorly completed job, there's no reason why it should be destructive or shatter a person's confidence.

Accepting compliments

How do you react when someone comments on an outfit you're wearing and tells you how good you look? Do you ever:

- blush and say nothing?
- wave your hand dismissively and say, *'Oh, I just picked it up in a sale'*?
- rush to reply, *'Well your dress really suits you too'*?

Now imagine the scenario in reverse. Suppose you were to tell a friend how smart she looked in her new suit and she responded in one of those ways. How would you feel then? Snubbed? Hurt? Wish you hadn't bothered saying anything?

Recognise and acknowledge a compliment when you're paid one. It's very simple to do and it saves a great deal of embarrassment and bad feeling on both sides. Next time someone tells you that you look great or congratulates you on a piece of work, try saying: *'Thanks, I'm glad you like it'* or *'Thanks, that's made me feel great'*, or *'Thanks, I really worked hard on that job.'*

Giving praise

We all have a need to be loved and wanted, to have our contributions recognised, to be congratulated on our achievements. Yet praise is a very underused resource. When was the last time you complimented or congratulated a partner, friend or colleague? Think about how good you feel when someone pays *you* a compliment or praises something *you've* done. Now think about how you feel when you don't receive praise when you think you deserve it. Remember that others feel like this too, so don't withhold those compliments.

Give praise:

- When it's due and give it often.
- Immediately. There's no point in waiting until well after the event to offer your congratulations — it just won't sound the same.
- Sincerely. Praise only what you think is worth praising, otherwise the recipient will have little respect for your compliments.

Taking criticism

Let's have a look at how our friends Aggressive Aggie, Passive Petula and Manipulative Minnie react to criticism. Imagine that all three have just been criticised by a colleague for the way they carried out a particular task. Here are their responses:

Aggressive Aggie storms around the office *'How dare you suggest I'm incompetent? If anyone's incompetent around here it's you. Just wait until you get a similar job, see what sort of support you get from me then...'*

Passive Petula looks doleful *'I just can't help it. I'm always making mistakes. It's not my fault I'm not as bright as you. This department would be a lot better off without me...'*

Manipulative Minnie goes on the defence *'Look this isn't fair. It's not my fault everything went wrong, why pick on me? I didn't have enough information...'*

Aggressive Aggie pretends she's impervious to criticism and goes on the attack; she has to 'win'. Manipulative Minnie also refuses to acknowledge that there may be a grain of truth in the criticism; instead her sense of injustice comes bubbling out as she searches for a scapegoat. As for Passive Petula, criticism is yet another nail in her coffin; she automatically accepts and takes to heart whatever is levelled at her. Do you see any parallels in your own behaviour?

Before you begin to deal assertively with criticism, you need to understand something about yourself. It's especially important to recognise your **crumple zones**.

Why is it that you can make the same remark to two different people and while one shrugs it off, the other directs a tirade at you. Kerry is a very attractive woman, yet every time you greet her with the words, 'You're looking well', she replies somewhat disgruntled, 'Really?' A bizarre response until you learn that Kerry is very sensitive about her shape and equates the words, 'you look really well' with 'you've put on weight'.

In the deepest, darkest recesses of our brain we hide our

54

sensitivities – sometimes we don't even admit them to ourselves. They only rear their heads when we over-react in some way to an otherwise innocent comment. These are our crumple zones. They may be about our appearance – the shape of our nose, state of our skin or figure or our abilities and skills or about background, race or class. Learn to recognise your crumple zones. Next time a friend comments that you seem over-sensitive or a little uptight about a remark, ask yourself, 'Has someone just stepped on my crumple zone?'

In order to handle criticism assertively, you need to recognise what sort of criticism it is. Before you fly off the handle and deny or make excuses for whatever it is you've been criticised about, stop for one moment and think, 'Is it true?' Hard as it may seem, if there's an inkling of justification in the criticism, then acknowledge it. This doesn't mean you have to eat humble pie or belittle yourself. Don't be afraid of apologising or admitting you've made a mistake.

Each term Belinda has to complete an essay for her college course. Her tutor asked Belinda to come and see him, and said: *'Belinda, I'm very disappointed by your latest essay. It's badly researched, poorly argued and full of spelling mistakes. It looks as though you didn't take much time preparing it.'* Belinda realises the criticism is valid and she answers assertively: *'Yes, I can see you're disappointed. I left it until the last minute and didn't have time to research it properly. You're right, I wrote it in a hurry and didn't check it through. I should have taken more care. I'll try to plan my next essay well in advance.*

Sometimes you realise the criticism is valid, but you're satisfied with what you have said or done and you feel an apology or change in your behaviour is inappropriate.

Erica's mother, who has different ideas about dress sense, criticises her: *Erica, you always look such a scruff with those torn jeans and clodhopping boots.*
Erica replies: *Yes, I know I look scruffy, but I like this look and I feel comfortable.*

When you're confronted with criticism which you know to be completely untrue, how often do you start trying to make the accusation fit? A friend tells you that you're selfish, but you know that you're not a selfish person. If you begin scanning your past life to find a single selfish act, you may well find yourself accepting her criticism even though, rationally thinking, it is not valid.

If the criticism isn't legitimate, then say so.

Chris is in a morose mood and starts criticising his girlfriend Penny:

> Chris: *Honestly I don't think you care about me. You're always out and about with your friends, you never spend time with me.*
>
> Penny: *Chris that's completely untrue. I do care about you. We've spent every weekend together.'*

Don't apologise for rejecting an invalid criticism, respond with conviction. You might try a phrase such as: *'That's simply not true,'* or *'On the contrary...,'* or *'I don't accept that at all...'*

Put downs are hard to define, except by saying that they are usually irrelevant, mean and worthless. The sort of comments that are labelled as put downs are phrases such as: *'Your problem is you can't take a joke'*, *'Women, they're all alike'*, or *'That's just what I'd expect from you'*. They are never intended to say anything constructive, but may well be intended to bait you. So how do you deal with them? Ideally you come up with some biting, witty remark. The only problem is, that's easier said than done. The best policy, therefore, is to ignore them. If you're subjected to a barrage of put downs by one particular individual then consider taking the time at a later, more appropriate date, to confront that person and say how you feel about their comments.

What sort of criticism?

Sometimes it's hard to know whether the criticism is actually valid or not, or if it's just a put down. Help yourself find out by questioning the person who's criticising you. You can do this by using what's known as negative enquiries and statements.

Here are some examples of negative statements.

- I find it hard to tackle details.
- I've been really preoccupied lately.
- I talk a lot when I get nervous.
- I know I'm inconsistent.

and negative enquiries:

- Are you dissatisfied with the quality of my work?
- Do you feel I'm pushing you into doing things you'd rather not do?
- Do you feel I could have been more supportive?
- Are you angry with me?

By putting the two elements together you can open up the way to a more frank and constructive discussion. For example: *'I've been really preoccupied lately. Do you feel I could have been more supportive?'* or *'I know I'm inconsistent. Does this make you angry?'*

This technique is also useful for those situations where you think the other person is trying to tell you something about your personality or behaviour but doesn't know what to say to you.

Giving constructive criticism

Giving criticism can be akin to treading on eggshells. How can you be positive, constructive *and* leave the other person's ego intact? There are six vital elements to remember:

1 *Get straight to the point.*
We discussed this earlier in this chapter, under Saying 'No'. Don't beat around the bush and prolong the agony.

2 *Describe the behaviour, don't label the person.*
Avoid labelling someone as clumsy or boring or selfish. Labels

have a habit of becoming self fulfilling. Instead of saying, *'You're so clumsy. Why did you drop my Ming vase?'* try instead, *'I thought it was clumsy of you to drop my Ming vase.'* Dropping your vase on the floor is a clumsy act; it does not automatically mean that the person who dropped it is always clumsy.

3 *Express your feelings.*
As with any kind of request or statement, it's important to say how you feel. Let the other person know where you stand. This way you avoid the complexities of, *'Well who does she think she is, telling me off...'* etc.

4 *Highlight positive qualities.*
This doesn't mean search around desperately for something nice to say. It does mean highlight behaviour or actions which you'd like to see more of (in contrast to that which you're criticising). For example, *'I really appreciated your help when... because....'*

5 *Be specific.*
If you think something is wrong or could be improved, then you need to let the other person know what it is you expect of them and the consequences if it doesn't happen. You might also want to suggest how they may make the changes you want to see.

6 *Let the other person speak!*
You must let the other person have the opportunity to express how they feel, to accept the criticism or not. If you don't, you might find yourself barking up completely the wrong tree:

Cindy was becoming increasingly cross that her new secretary, Pam, didn't seem to be getting through her work and, assuming that she was just wasting time, took her to task. The real reason for the delay was that Pam was unfamiliar with the word processing package and it was taking her time to get up to speed. It wasn't until the end of the meeting that Pam managed to put her side of the story. It took some time to repair relations between the two.

For more about how to listen, see the next section, page 60.

Let's put all these elements together.

Lesley and Muriel have an arrangement to do their weekly shop together using Lesley's car. For the past three weeks Muriel has turned up late. This throws Lesley's day out so she decides to tackle Muriel. This is how the conversation goes:

Lesley: *Muriel, it's half past ten. We agreed to meet at ten. I feel really put out when you turn up late. Is there any reason why you can't make it earlier?*

Muriel: *Er, no. I just can't seem to get out of the house, what with trying to make a shopping list.*

Lesley: *When you came on time we managed to miss the worst of the rush which meant we finished much quicker. I'd appreciate it if you could be here at ten sharp. Why don't you write out your shopping list the night before?*

Muriel: *Look, I'll try.*

Lesley: *I intend to leave at ten next week, so if you're here you're welcome to a lift, otherwise I shall go without you.*

Giving criticism is often one of the least comfortable tasks. For this reason, it's a perfect candidate for a well thought out survival script, see pages 62–65.

Help yourself to handle criticism

1 Make a list of all your crumple zones. Practise acknowledging them. Begin your acknowledgement, *'Yes, I am...'*

2 Think over the last time someone paid you a compliment. How did you react? Were you assertive? If not, how could you have responded?

3 Make a list of people you love or admire. When was the last time you paid them a compliment or offered your praise? Plan what you could say − and go and say it!

4 Try making a spontaneous gesture or statement of appreciation in the next day or two.

LEARNING TO LISTEN

Listening is a vital part of the communication process.

How do you feel when you're talking to someone and you're pretty sure they're not listening to you? Frustrated? Alone? With a few dents in your self-esteem? We spend a lot of time hearing what other people say but failing to listen properly. And when we do listen we tend to forget what we've heard. We're all too busy trying to get in our own pennyworth or simply daydreaming about something quite different. Listening properly and assertively to what other people are saying means being able to understand what they are really trying to tell you, encouraging them to open up, and ensuring that your response, if it's called for, is appropriate.

There are three ways you can help yourself to listen assertively:

Listen with your whole body.

Your ears are only one part of your listening mechanism. You know how frustrating it is to try to talk to someone while they're staring out of the window or watching TV. How can you be sure you're getting your message across if you haven't got their full attention? Make sure your body indicates you're willing to listen.

- Don't hunch up protectively. Lean forward, keen to hear what they have to say.
- Maintain eye contact. Look back to Assertive Body Talk, pages 26–36.
- Cut out other distractions − noise, TV, phones ringing.

Listen to help others to talk.

How often have you sensed that someone was out of sorts? They haven't actually said anything, but you know from the expression on their face that something's up. Instead of telling them to 'Snap out of it', which may have precisely the opposite effect, you can encourage them to open up.

- Describe their behaviour: *'You look very pleased with yourself'* or *'You seem rather upset.'*
- Invite them to talk: *'Do you want to talk about it?'* or encourage them to keep talking: *'Please go on, I'll listen.'*
- Keep quiet and let the other person decide whether they want to talk and if so what they want to say. Never bully someone into talking to you.
- Use very brief prompts to indicate your willingness to listen. The most common one is 'mm-hmm'. You could also try *'Go on'*, *'I see'*, *'Oh?'*, *'really?'*, *'then'*?
- You could also try asking questions. See pages 69–70.

Once the speaker gets going it's best simply to shut up and listen.

Good listening means responding.

This doesn't mean throwing in any old remark. Nor does it mean taking over the entire conversation so that you end up discussing you rather than the other person. There are three ways you can respond to show the speaker that you've understood and accepted what they've said. Remember, good listeners don't sit in judgement.

First, you can help the speaker to sum up what they've said.

Katy: *Mum, I don't know what to do. I've had this job offer, it's well paid and it sounds really exciting, but it means dropping out of college. I like college, I want to get a good qualification but, I don't know, perhaps I should take the job.*

Mum: *Seems that you're torn both ways, you've got a chance to take up a great job but you want college life and qualifications.*

Katy: *Yes.*

A simple nod from the speaker is usually enough to tell you you're on the right track and it saves any misunderstandings.

Secondly, you can help the speaker summarise their feelings:

Marianne: *This job is great. I'm really enjoying the work. The only thing that gets me down is that I'm so far away from my friends.*

Denise: *Sounds as if, even though the job's going so well, you're feeling a bit low.*

Thirdly, you can help the speaker focus on what they've been saying and begin to see the wood for the trees:

Over five cups of coffee Rita has been recalling a catalogue of her life's disasters to her friend Carol. She thinks her husband is having an affair, she's worried that she's losing her looks, she wants to try and get out of the house and find a job. By the sixth cup of coffee Rita's in a dejected heap. Carol's got one eye on the clock and she's expecting her kids to arrive home at any moment, so she helps Rita to focus on her problems: *'Rita, you're worried that Bob might be having an affair, but you don't know for sure. You recognise you're not getting any younger and think you're less attractive. But you also want to do something with your life, find a job, get out of the house.'*

Focusing can help you move the conversation on. If you don't, you might just find yourself listening to the same ever-circling story which won't get you — or the speaker — anywhere.

Help yourself to listen

1 Sit in front of a mirror. Practise open listening postures. Watch what you do with your arms, don't cross them.

2 Think back over the last conversation you had with someone. How did you react? What sort of phrases did you respond with? Do you think they felt comfortable talking to you?

3 Next time you're listening to someone be very aware of your behaviour. When the conversation is over, find out from them whether they felt you were listening fully to them. Obviously it's best to get feedback from someone you know well — a stranger might feel a bit embarrassed!

How to write
A survival script

Have you ever thought to yourself, 'If only I'd known what to say', or kicked yourself for being caught off guard by someone else's surprise response? Be prepared — write yourself a survival script.

The aim of writing a survival script is to give you the chance to work out what you want to say in advance. It also gives you the opportunity to imagine how the other person might respond and how in turn you would reply to them. It's a way of helping you feel more comfortable with a situation, particularly one which you might see as potentially difficult.

A survival script needs four elements:

- a description of where and when the meeting or confrontation takes place;
- something about the other person or people;
- what you're going to say;
- how the other person might react and how you would respond.

To be of any use, your survival script must be realistic. To achieve this you need to recognise your worst nightmares and get them into a sensible perspective.

Jenny lent her friend Marianne £100 three months ago. Marianne promised to pay the money back within a fortnight. She didn't and Jenny needs the money, but she's embarrassed to ask for it. She lies awake in bed at night tossing and turning. Here are some of Jenny's night-time monsters: Marianne will deny Jenny ever lent her the money; Marianne will just laugh and say she thought it was a gift; Marianne will storm off and never speak to her again.

Once you've made a list of all those imaginary monsters, you need to get a grip on the situation. Ask yourself two questions: in real life, what's the worst that's likely to happen? What would I do if it did?

Jenny has a more rational think. She decides that the worst that's likely to happen is for Marianne to go off in a huff and take her time about paying up. Jenny reminds herself that she has every right to ask her friend to return the loan and to do so quickly. She decides that she is not prepared to let this incident ruin her friendship, but if Marianne takes offence then so be it.

Now you've thought about the worst possible outcome and decided what you would do if it happened, you're ready to start drafting your survival script.

1 Where and when?
To help yourself to feel more comfortable, imagine where and when the meeting is going to take place. Obviously you won't always be able to do this, for example if you're going to an unfamiliar building for a job interview. However, you can think back to other similar situations, how the room was set out, how you felt. One of the reasons for thinking about the time and place is so that, if you are able to, you can change them if you think they're inappropriate. Remember, the venue can have an important effect on what you say; see page 51.

Jenny considers inviting Marianne over for supper in the evening but then she thinks again. She decides she wants to be business-like about the loan and so it would be better to meet her friend somewhere neutral. Jenny's script looks something like this:

Setting the scene: asking Marianne to repay my loan. Meet in the Town Wine Bar at the back where it's quiet, lunchtime. Buy drinks and order something to eat first.

2 Who?

Think about what you know about the other person. Try to judge their mood and how they might feel about this situation.

Who? Marianne, one of my oldest and closest friends. She can be very off-hand about other people's feelings — and their property. I don't imagine she's even thought I might feel embarrassed about asking for the money back. Tends to be very slapdash about things. Hates people making a fuss over trivial things — probably thinks this is trivial.

3 What to say?

If you're spending an entire day or afternoon with someone, you obviously don't want to script every moment of your meeting — just concentrate on those things which are bothering you. Look back to the beginning of this chapter, Making Requests, to remind yourself about how to make an assertive request. Don't forget to describe what's wrong, be specific and direct and express your feelings. If it's appropriate you might also want to say what will happen if your reqest isn't met.
 Jenny writes out what she wants to say:

Marianne, three months ago I lent you £100. You promised to pay it back within a fortnight, but you haven't. I feel very embarrassed about asking for it, but I need the money urgently and I'd like it back this afternoon.

4 Consider the responses

This is about ensuring — as far as you can — that you don't get caught out. Think of all the things the other person might say, or how they might react. For each statement or act, script how you would respond.
 Jenny thinks Marianne might respond with two comments:

Marianne: *Oh Jenny, ease up, it's only £100, you can't be that desperate. You'll get it back, stop worrying.*

Jenny: *I know you don't think this is a big deal but to me £100 is a lot of money. I need it urgently. I'd like it returned this afternoon.*

Marianne: *I just can't lay my hands on it right now.*
[Excuses follow]

Jenny: *How much can you give me this afternoon? When will you be able to return the rest?*

Jenny resolves not to let the matter drop. She decides to set a time for the money to be returned and if necessary to go with Marianne to the bank.

Think through your options carefully — right to their conclusions.

With time, writing a survival script is something you can learn to do in your head. If you have a really big event or difficult situation coming up, it's worth taking a few minutes to sit down quietly and commit your survival script to paper. For some more examples see Chapter 6.

Help yourself to write a survival script

Think back over a recent confrontation. With hindsight, write a survival script for that situation. Do you think the outcome could have been any different?

4

More Assertion Techniques

Becoming assertive means more positive interactions with others
– whether on a speaking platform, at a job interview, or in bed.
Here are some extra tips for those special occasions!

SOCIAL SAVVY

Dinner for eight, cocktails at six, wild partying into the night.
What's your response to a social invitation? Do you grab it with
glee and think, what fun, maybe I'll meet some wonderful new
people? Or do you see it as a gruesome ordeal? Are you the sort
of person who spends the entire evening hovering round the
sausage rolls hoping someone suave and fascinating will come
and talk to you, terrified all the same that it might just happen.
Or do you find a friend and cling like a limpet to them throughout the entire proceedings?

Social and business gatherings, whether they're a local PTA
meeting, a lunch for two or the launch of your firm's latest
product can cause untold misery. What am I going to do all
evening? Who am I going to talk to? What am I going to talk
about? What if I can't think of anything to say? Don't worry,
you're not alone. If it's any consolation, you can bet that at least
ten other people in the room feel exactly as you do!

There's an art to making conversation and it's one you can learn. But like all things, first you must believe in yourself. The more you practise meeting and talking to people, the more confident you'll be and the more pleasurable and profitable socialising will become. Don't lose out because you feel dumbstruck — there's always someone to talk to and something to talk about! Make a Rights Charter for social interaction.

- I have the right to talk to people I don't know.
- I have the right to say what I think.
- I have the right to feel nervous when I meet people for the first time.
- I have the right to end a conversation.

Top tips for social savvy

1 *Make your entrance*
Smile, be open, be warm. Make people want to spend time with you, invite conversation. A friendly hallo, a firm handshake and good eye contact give positive signals. They tell others you're a nice person, you're interested in what they have to say, you want to spend time with them.

2 *Stop playing the 'I think, you think, I think' game*
This is the one where you spend the entire evening thinking, 'They all think I'm stupid, boring and have fat legs'. Disappointing as it might be, if you've merged into the sausage rolls, no one's probably given you a single thought. Stop thinking about yourself.

3 *Start being interested not interesting*
If you concentrate every ounce of your energy on trying to create a good impression, you'll end up with quite the opposite effect. Stop attempting to make yourself interesting and start being interested in others and what they have to say. Good conversationalists are the ones who know how to react, not act.

4 *You can talk to anyone*
How many times have you been introduced to someone and

thought, 'What on earth am I going to say to him – I can't imagine we've got a thing in common.' The only reason you don't think you've got anything to talk about is because you don't know anything about that person. Put aside your first impressions – don't be misled by what the person looks like, what they're wearing, their job title. Find out more: *'I've never met an actuary before – tell me, what do you do?'* And even if their job isn't scintillating they still live somewhere, go on holiday, eat food, watch TV. You don't need to like the same things and have identical views to talk to another person. And don't dismiss people because you don't immediately regard them as a future best buddy, mate or business contact – you never know!

5 *Make your introduction work*
The worst way to introduce yourself is to say simply, 'Hi, I'm Jane'. It's the surest way of ending a conversation before it's begun. Tell your partner more about you, give them something to respond to, try saying, *'Hi, I'm Jane, I'm a good friend of Louise's. We both work at the library and I live round the corner'*, or *'Hallo, I'm Sarah Hamilton, I'm a solicitor, I work in local government.'*

6 *Promote your friends and colleagues*
When you introduce two people, boost their self-esteem, make it easier for them to start and keep up a conversation. Instead of saying, 'Tania meet Jacky – I'll leave you to get to know each other', try: *'Tania, let me introduce Jacky, one of my dearest friends. We go back a long way, she's a brilliant business woman – she imports incredible pottery from Italy. Tania has just started out on her own making wonderful jewellery, so I'm sure you'll have a lot to talk about.'*

7 *Plan your ice-breakers*
What do you say when someone sidles up to you at the buffet table or stands next to you powdering their nose in the ladies? There are four good standbys.

Compliments – not chat-up lines – are always great:
   'I couldn't help noticing your brooch, it's so pretty. Did you buy it abroad?'

'The tie you're wearing, it's got an impressive emblem — has it any special significance?'

'I really enjoyed the speech you made, particularly your comment about...'

A positive comment about the event you're attending. (Don't be rude, you don't know who you're talking to):

'This is a great party, Veronica's a wonderful hostess.'

'What do you think about the new product?'

'Have you tried this salad, it's got very interesting nuts in it.'

News:

'What do you think of the latest events in...'

'I saw the news before I came out, I was really shocked by the pictures of...'

'Did you see that photograph of...'

The old standbys:

'I love all this sunshine we're having, have you had a chance to enjoy it?'

'Have you come far, or do you live locally?'

And failing all that, why not try, *'Hallo, I'm ..., I'm new to this area, I don't know a soul here, you seem to be on first-name terms with everyone, I'd appreciate it if you could introduce me.'*

8 *Use all the free information you can get*

Even if someone hasn't actually said much to you, there's always plenty of 'free information' around to help you keep the conversation going. Free information can include nonverbal clues, what the person's wearing — the compliment ice-breaker above is a good example — or whether they have an accent or perhaps that they are soaking wet from head to foot! It also includes information that they give you which you haven't requested. For example: *'Gosh, your shoes look soaking wet. How far have you had to come?' 'Well, actually there was a bomb scare at the station and I had to walk most of the way.'* At this point you've a choice; you can talk about bomb scares — your experiences, the politics of it all, etc, or find out where the other person's come from — or both.

9 *Ask open-ended questions*

There are two ways to ask a question. You can ask closed questions, such as '*Do you like your job?*' which usually elicit simple 'yes' or 'no' answers and therefore do little to help you build the conversation. Or you can use open-ended questions, which achieve the opposite. An open-ended question involves asking how, or what, or why. For example, you could say, '*What do you enjoy most about your job?*' or '*Why did you choose that profession?*'

10 *Share information about yourself*

This doesn't mean droning on for hours about your life, your fears and your ambitions. It does mean sharing information about yourself with the other person. If you want a relationship to develop you have to be prepared to tell the other person about yourself — and vice versa. Learn to share your views, your likes and dislikes, your feelings.

11 *Build your conversation*

Keeping a conversation going is a bit like building a brick wall. You use each layer of information you get to build another one. Once you find a topic you're both interested in, don't let it wither, elaborate on what you've said.

> You: *Have you tried this pizza, it's excellent.*
>
> Him: *Not yet. Actually since I've moved to the area I've been trying to find a decent Italian restaurant.*
>
> You: *Oh, there's a great one on the High Street, Luigi's, it does some amazing home-made pasta. It's got a great atmosphere, too. Lots of clutter and noise, the football on in the corner. It's just like being in Italy — have you ever been there?*
>
> Him: *I've been to Florence. It's a very romantic place and I love the art and architecture.*
>
> You: *What did you think of. . .*

Practise describing the places you're talking about. Make the other person feel they've been there too. And don't be afraid of silences, you don't need to fill every moment with chat.

12 *Know how and when to take your leave*

There comes a point when all good conversations flag or the witching hour strikes and it's time to retire. Know when and how to take your leave. If you've been trying to strike up a conversation with a person but they seem to be more interested in searching out someone else you could say: '*I can see you're preoccupied so I'll leave you to your friends/colleagues.*'

Or perhaps the conversation has reached its natural end: '*I'm very glad to have met you, I've enjoyed our talk. Perhaps we'll meet again later.*' Or then again, you might be desperate to move on: '*It was nice to meet you; well I think I'd better go and mingle/there's someone I want to talk to now.*'

If you like the person and want to see them again, let them know. You'll soon find out whether the feeling is mutual. You could try: '*I really enjoyed meeting you. Perhaps we could continue our conversation another day?*' or '*Before I go, here's my number/business card, do get in touch, it would be great to hear from you again*' or '*I'm glad I had the chance to talk to you. Would you like to meet again next week? Do you want to make a date now or shall I call you?*'

ASSERTIVE SEX

We live in a society saturated with sex. From all sides we're bombarded with messages telling us what to do, how to do it and who to do it with. Yet for all the titillating of the tabloids and the plain speaking of the the problem pages the subject remains largely taboo. Bawdy jokes, hushed whispering in the girls' loos, innuendo in the bedroom. Is it any wonder that very many people engage in non-assertive sex?

Have you ever:

- Agreed to have sex even though you weren't in the mood or didn't fancy the other person?
- Wanted sex but didn't say so?
- Used sex to bargain for something?

Consider what the word sex means to you. Do you think of it as fun or a bore, loving or indifferent, mutual or selfish, exciting or deadly, passionate or mechanical, something to look forward to or something to be endured? Does sex delight you or do you dread it?

Sex is another form of communication. It's a means of expressing love and desire, of relieving tension, of seeking reassurance and of maintaining physical and emotional wellbeing. But sex also has its negative side. Of all the ways to communicate it is the one most riddled with guilt, ignorance, discomfort and dishonesty.

From sixteen to ninety-six, sex is what you make it. It's up to you to make the choices. Only you can decide what you want to do, how you want to do it and who you want to do it with. Like anything else, sex is on a lifetime's learning curve. Your desires and opportunities change over the years. Assertive sex is satisfying, fulfilling and mutual. There are no limits on what you can or can't do, so long as you and, if appropriate, your partner feel comfortable with your choices. Make a Rights Charter for your sex life:

- I have the right to determine my own sexuality.
- I have the right to make sexual demands.
- I have the right to refuse sex.
- I have the right to gain sexual pleasure.

And here are your top tips for assertive sex:

Top tips to assertive sex

1 *Find out how your body works*
Don't be afraid to ask for information about sex and sexuality. If you missed out on school biology lessons, make an opportunity to find out how your body functions. There are plenty of good, straightforward books around. Use them to inform, educate and maybe even to inspire!

2 *Discover the sense of touch*

Many people shy away from physical contact, often because they were denied hugs and kisses as children. If you don't feel comfortable with your body, get to know it better. Invest in a bottle of really wonderful smelling aromatherapy oil and give yourself a good all over massage. For the best effect, try it after a warm bath. Why not offer your partner a soothing massage and get him to do the same for you?

3 *Express your feelings*

Learning to express your feelings is the key to becoming assertive, regardless of what you are doing. But it's particularly crucial as far as sex is concerned. Sex, perhaps more than any other aspect of life, relies a great deal on intense passion, touch and fumblings in the dark. Is it surprising that in the embarrassment of grunts and groans and general anatomical groping people become dissatisfied, frightened or frustrated? Whether you want sex or you don't want sex or you want sex in a particular way, tell your partner:

'I'm worried about AIDS, I'm not prepared to have sex without using a condom.'
'I feel really uncomfortable about having sex with the light on, I'd prefer to switch it off.'
'I've never had sex before, I feel nervous.'
'I always feel tense with a new partner.'
'I really enjoy sitting astride you/with you on top/side by side...'
'I've got my period but I feel quite comfortable having sex if you do too.'
'I feel really hurt when you turn over and go off to sleep as soon as we finish making love.'

4 *Ask for what you want*

Who decides what you do in bed, or anywhere else for that matter? Does your partner know what turns you on or do you hope he'll hit the right spot by accident? Look at it this way, if you don't tell your partner what gives you satisfaction, how on earth is he supposed to guess? But the reverse is equally true.

Have you taken the time to find out what gives your partner pleasure? You don't need to go into deep discussions, you could say simply:

'Do you like me touching/rubbing/stroking/licking you here ... or do you prefer me touching/rubbing/stroking/licking you here?' and moving your hand, tongue or whatever as necessary.

By the same token move your partner's hand or body to where it gives you pleasure. Even saying one word such as, *'higher'* or *'lower'*, *'harder'* or *'softer'* can make all the difference. Acknowledge things that give you pleasure. Straightforward grunts or moans usually suffice or you could say: *'Mm, that's really nice'* or *'that really turns me on.'*

5 Do what gives you pleasure
Sex is about fun and frolics, entertainment and enjoyment. There are no rules and regulations about what constitutes a good time. Earlier in the book we discussed positive thinking and looked at the small voices that ring in our heads. What does your small voice say about sex? Does it frown sternly just when you feel your body begin to tingle, reminding you that there are more important things to be done, telling you to keep quiet, not romp around, to slow down or hurry up? Accept that you have the right to discover what gives you pleasure and to enjoy it.

6 Take the lead
The myth says that men, not women, initiate sex. What nonsense. Take responsibility for your own sex drive. If you want sex, say so, express your feelings. Don't fear rejection. If you partner says no, respect his response.

7 Don't say yes to sex if you mean no
Why do women submit to sex when they'd rather go to sleep, read a book, just cuddle or simply don't fancy the male in question? There are many reasons: fear of rejection or losing their partner; fear of being thought frigid or a tease; an assumption that it's their duty as a wife or girlfriend; or the pay-off at the end of an evening out. Added to all these is the great male erection myth. Let's deflate this one immediately. Men with erections will not explode or come to harm if they don't find relief. A man's erection is not your responsibility.

Let's look at two common situations where you might want to say no to sex.

Man and woman have just been out on a date. After coffee at woman's flat, they reach the 'to bed or not to bed' stage. This is what happens:

Woman: *Thanks for a great evening. It's late so let's call it a day.*

Man: *You know I think you're incredibly attractive, you really turn me on.*

Woman: *Thanks, but it is late and I'd appreciate it if you could leave now.*

Man: *Come on, why don't we get into bed?*

Woman: *I don't want sex with you, I think it's time for you to go.*

Man: *What's the matter with you, you're turning into a right tease. What are you, frigid?*

Woman: *That was unnecessary. I'm not prepared to argue. Please will you leave.*

In the second scenario, man and woman have been together for a number of years. Woman is tired and doesn't feel like sex. Non-assertive reactions might be to snap back, 'Stop groping at me' or start a row, or pretend to be asleep, or have a headache, or discuss a problem about the central heating. An assertive response might be:

Woman: *I'm really tired, I don't feel like making love tonight.*

Man: *Come on, just a quick one.*

Woman: *No, I'm exhausted. I don't want sex but I'd really like you to hold me close.*

8 *Don't underestimate the power of a cuddle*
Full-blown sex isn't the only way to express love and affection. A hug, stroking, gentle kissing and a long and luxuriating cuddle can be far more effective. If you just want to get in touch with your partner with reassurance rather than passion, say so and snuggle up. Make it clear, it doesn't have to lead to anything else.

9 *Never bargain with sex*

Withholding or agreeing to sex in order to get something you want or because you're angry or frustrated is definitely out of bounds. Sex is not a threat with which to bully someone into submission, nor is it a reward for good behaviour. Sex in these circumstances becomes empty, callous and ultimately unsatisfying for one or both partners.

10 *Bed is not the place to discuss your sex life*

If you really want to talk about your sex life, don't do it in bed. If you want to criticise or confront your partner constructively, then doing so while you're lying horizontally, possibly naked, back to back and with the light out, is not going to get assertive results! Choose your time and place carefully. Don't make your bed a battleground.

FEEL SAFE, BE SAFE

Attacks on women are the bread and butter of daily news bulletins. Is it any wonder that a message is getting through — women simply aren't safe.

How many of your female friends and acquaintances have modified their life-styles because of their fear of violence? Women who won't go out at night, women barricaded in their cars and homes, women who are frightened to walk around their neighbourhood estates in the middle of the afternoon or use public transport, women who think twice about working late or getting into a lift alone. And this is supposed to be the era of the independent, liberated, female.

Feeling safe, and acting safe, is about believing in yourself and following sensible precautions. It means taking stock of your nightmare of unspecified horrors and transforming them into something practical and positive. It also means moving away from the little-girl-lost, doubting victim to the assertive equal. This isn't about being cocky. Wandering through a deserted park at night is plain stupid. It is about getting the balance right. Don't lose out on life because you're afraid to move from A to

B. Learn to recognise the danger and learn to protect yourself.

Safe women cannot afford to be nice women. Most individuals who attack women are looking for an easy target. Assertive women are not easy targets. To get the situation into perspective, remember that three-quarters of women who experience violence do so at the hands of someone they know. There are plenty of books and courses on self-protection and self-defence. Use them to find out more about how you can help yourself and boost your self-confidence. But remember, however sophisticated the whistle or the armlock, it's no substitute for your best defence resource − your belief in yourself. Make a Rights Charter for your personal safety:

- I have the right to feel safe at home and work.
- I have the right not to be intimidated when I'm out.
- I have the right to walk tall along the street.
- I have the right to take steps to protect myself without feeling silly.
- I have the right to ask for help if I feel I'm in danger.
- I have the right to be rude and shout loudly at someone whose behaviour I find threatening.
- I have the right to take the risk of offending someone who meant me no harm.

Top tips to feeling safe

1 *Make your home safe*
This doesn't mean that you have to turn your home into a fortress. There are very simple steps you can take to ensure your home isn't an easy target for burglars and prowlers − whether you're in or not. The Crime Prevention Officer at your local police station will be able to give you plenty of practical advice.

Ensure your front door and path are always well lit at night. Use a porch light on a timer or install lights that automatically come on as soon as someone approaches the house. This applies to garages and back alleys, anywhere that you might have to stop and get out of a car or open a door. And always have your keys ready. If you come home after dark, fit timers on lamps in your living-room or bedroom. This not only leads others to think there's someone at home, it also means you don't have to walk into a pitch black house. Never put your name on a doorbell, especially if it signals loud and clear to everyone that you're a woman on her own. The same applies to listings in telephone directories and advertisements in newspapers or newsagents. Keep a phone by you at night. Try to get one that you can pre-program with a neighbour's number and your local police station. Get to know your neighbours. If you don't know who's living near you, you won't know if they can help you in an emergency.

2 *Be doorwise*

If you're not sure who's at the door, then ask, or open the door with the security chain on. Never invite strangers into your home however plausible their excuse. If someone comes collecting for charity and you haven't got any cash to hand, shut the door firmly while you find some. Genuine collectors, male or female, will accept this as quite normal.

What do you do if someone comes banging on your door desperate to call the police because there's been an accident? You don't have to open the door. Ask them for the briefest details and say you'll call the police.

3 *Don't land yourself up a blind alley*

Never embark on a journey, especially one that involves going somewhere unpopulated, with a reputation for violence or where you're going to be travelling in the dark, without thinking it through first. How are you going to get there — and back? Do you know exactly where you are going, have you a map? Have you got a telephone number in case you get lost? What happens if you can't get a train or bus? Have you got enough petrol?

Always find out bus and train timetables so that you don't have to wait around at an empty bus or train station. Find out which stops are busier and alter your journey if possible. Taxis may be more expensive than public transport or walking, but they're much safer. Always phone for a licensed taxi or minicab and ask for the registration number and the driver's name and description. Never, ever, pick up a minicab on the street. Always park near the entrance to a multistorey car park. Ask the attendant if there's a space — most will be very sympathetic. Don't ever take short cuts if you don't know exactly where they lead to. And don't take short cuts across parks or open spaces unless they are full of people.

4 *Walk streetwise*
Confident body language is vital out on the street or in any unfamiliar situation. Make sure you look as if you mean business. Don't let bad posture give away non-assertive vibes — even if your heart is thumping inside. If you look confident and walk purposefully, you are far less likely to become a victim. Look back Assertive Body Talk, pages 26–36.

5 *Be streetwise*
Most of us sense when something's not right. Go with your gut reaction. If you think someone is following you, cross the street, see what happens and cross back if necessary. If you're frightened, then run. Look for escape routes — a pub or shop, or if necessary a well-lit doorway you can stop in.

Don't give people the benefit of the doubt. Take the risk of offending someone who meant you no harm. Rather a bruised ego than bruises or worse on you. Don't walk into trouble. If you see a gang of youths, cross the road, take another route, don't run straight into them.

Get your priorities right. If a thief grabs your handbag and makes off down a dark alley, let it go. Remember, material goods can be easily replaced — you can't.

6 *Dress safely*
There has been a huge debate about women 'inviting trouble' because of the way they dress. Many women feel, justifiably, they should be able to wear what they like without having to consider whether it might arouse male passions. That said, just think about this: if you walk along alone at night wearing a very short skirt, high heels and swinging a flimsy handbag what sort of signals do you send out? Well first, there's little mistaking you're a woman. Secondly, you're not very mobile or agile with your stilettos on. Thirdly, your bag is up for grabs — literally.

Throughout this book we've talked about being appropriate for the situation, whether it's how you make a request, express your anger — or what you wear. A low-cut minidress may be great for a party, but is it appropriate for walking back home once the party's over?

If you're out at night, try to look androgynous to the casual passer-by. Wear a long coat or cardigan over a short skirt, tuck your hair in and turn the collar up. Use a plain umbrella rather than a frilly, flowered one. If you wear high heels keep them for when you get to where you're going. Put on a pair of trainers or flat shoes so that you can walk quickly, or run if you have to. Try not to walk along with your hands full of shopping bags or other parcels. Rather use a larger handbag slung securely over one shoulder and across your body. Leave your hands free.

If you have a stranger such as a plumber or electrician visiting your house don't greet them in your satin negligee. Get dressed properly.

7 Ask for help

Don't be afraid of asking for help even if it's simply discussing your safety fears with flatmates, partners or colleagues. You may find that others feel the same way as you do. While just talking it through might make you feel better, you may also be able to do something practical together. If you're worried about getting to or from work or a social event, ask for a lift. Other women are likely to be extremely sympathetic. Even going about in twos and threes can feel much safer.

Practise asking for help, for example if you decide to take refuge in a shop or you move seats in a bus or train. You could say something like: *'I want to wait in your shop for a moment. A man has been following me down the road'* or *'Do you mind if I sit next to you? That man's behaviour is making me feel very uncomfortable.'*

8 Use your voice

If you find yourself in a threatening situation, perhaps being pestered by someone, use your voice. Don't whimper or whisper. Practise making your voice sound stronger. Draw out your words, speak louder and more deeply than you normally do. Try saying: '*Noow, goow awaay*', '*Leeve mee aloone*', '*Stopp touuching mee*'.

9 Set your own safety limits

Don't let other people dictate your safety levels. What may feel unthreatening to them, particularly if they're male, might make you feel very unsafe. Be assertive, don't push yourself up someone else's blind alley. You could say something like: '*I know you feel perfectly safe getting the last train home but I don't. I'd prefer to...*' or '*I know you think I'm daft not walking through the park in the afternoon, but it's empty and I don't feel safe. I prefer to take the longer route.*'

PERSUASIVE PRESENTATIONS

For many people there's nothing more terrifying than being called upon to make a speech or presentation. Whether you're talking to a small group of colleagues or addressing a thousand-strong conference, there's a point where even the most seasoned speaker gets the collywobbles. No matter how nervous you feel, you're not alone.

Close your eyes for a moment. Imagine yourself at a meeting in a room full of strangers. Imagine that you've just heard a very interesting talk and that you're dying to ask the speaker a question. Imagine that you put your hand up and the chairperson points to you and asks you to come up to the microphone. How do you feel at that very moment? What's going through your mind? Here are some common responses: I feel ... shaky, sick, dizzy, my mouth's dry; I think everyone's going to laugh at me ... my question's not important ... it's silly; I wonder why on earth I put my hand up; I worry my petticoat is showing ... that I'll trip up; my mind's gone blank ... I can't remember what it is I want to say ... I'll get my words mixed up; my voice is going to sound strained; they won't be able to hear me; I'll shout into the microphone; someone else could have put it over better than me.

Does that list ring any bells? All those responses taken

together read like a complete nightmare. But if you break them down, you'll find that they fall neatly into two categories. First, there are all the responses that are purely and simply about belief in yourself. These include the ones expressing fear that people will laugh, that your opinion isn't valid or the question important. Secondly, there are the responses that are to do with technique – how to project your voice and how to handle a microphone (see page 88).

The more experienced you become at putting across your view in public, the more confident you'll become. The two together mean that you're less likely to suffer from a paralysing attack of nerves. We all need to get the adrenalin going to give a good performance. What you don't want to happen, is for your nerves to get the better of you. How can you help yourself?

For a start, you need to work on your self-esteem, to learn to believe in yourself and to recognise that you have the right to make a contribution. You then need to learn how to help yourself keep your nerves at bay by understanding the tricks of speech making (see below). Preparation and practice are the keys to pulling off effective talks and presentations, so thirdly, use every opportunity you can to practise your presentation techniques – even if it's simply asking a question at a staff meeting, or volunteering to speak at a small business function or family gathering. Finally, if you're just starting out, take it slowly. Don't expect to stun the whole of the Royal Albert Hall on your first public appearance!

To give yourself an extra boost, pick up some clothes and make-up tips from Chapter 7, Looking Good, Feeling Good. Use the exercise on page 36 to help you calm those pre-presentation nerves. And if you have been asked to speak or make a presentation, congratulate yourself on accepting the offer. For many people the hardest part of all is actually saying 'yes'.

Make a Rights Charter for speaking out:

- I have the right to state my opinion.
- I have the right to have that opinion respected.
- I have the right to be listened to.
- I have the right to learn to be a polished speaker.

Top tips to making persuasive speeches and presentations

1 *Prepare!*
Before you attempt to commit even one word of your talk or presentation to paper, you need to consider:

● Your audience: Who are they? How many? How much do they know about the subject? What do you think they expect from you? Will they be friendly or hostile to what you have to say? What sort of language would be appropriate – formal or informal?
● Your aim: Why have you been invited? Is it to educate your audience, to persuade them to buy something or support a cause or take some action?

Once you've had a good think about your audience and why you're going to stand up in front of them, you'll have a much clearer idea of what you are going to say and how you are going to say it.

2 *Plan what you're going to say in advance*
Nobody but the most regular speakers with years of experience can talk off the cuff. If you haven't done it before, now's not the time to try. You need to plan word by word and line by line what you're going to say. And don't forget that even though you're writing down your presentation, ultimately you're going to speak it. Write your speech as if you were saying it in everyday language and avoid formal and tortuous prose.

3 *Grab your audience's attention*
When you begin, never ever waffle about the weather, the train journey or anything else. Thank your audience for coming and thank whoever introduced you for their introduction, then go straight in. If you've got a quotation or a startling statistic that will make your audience sit up – then use it. Always tell your audience what you're going to talk about.

'This morning I want to tell you about three things...'

*'Today I want to focus on four aspects of our work, one . . .
two . . . three and finally. . .'*
*'This evening I want to tell you about our new campaign, why
it was set up, what it hopes to achieve and how, I hope, you can
help us. . .'*

Make sure the main part of your presentation is interesting
and informative. And end with a really punchy remark.

4 Keep your audience with you
It's very easy to lose your audience's attention, especially if the
subject-matter is quite complex − or the speaker boring!
Never try to convey detailed points or statistics in your speech,
unless you have some kind of audio-visual back-up such as an
overhead projector and you've provided written fact sheets. It's
always better to leave this kind of information to a written
document for your audience to take away with them. Be kind to
your audience; no one likes to think that they haven't been
keeping up. Repeat your main points and use them to introduce
new ideas. Use anecdotes to illustrate what you are saying, but
sparingly. You don't want to turn your talk into your life story.
Suggest images and themes to stir your audience's imagination.
And if you can, involve your audience, throw questions out to
them.

5 Use your voice
Beware of falling into a monotone − it'll send your audience to
sleep. By varying the speed at which you speak, your tone,
inflections and pitch, you can easily make your presentation
much more interesting. Look back at Assertive Words, pages
25−26. Above all, be enthusiastic. Boring speakers soon make
their audience bored.
Most inexperienced speakers have a tendency to speak far too
fast − usually because, subconsciously or not, they want to get
the job over and done with as soon as possible. Slow down!
Don't be afraid of pausing to emphasise a point. Silence can be
strikingly effective.
If you tense your neck and you hunch your shoulders you will
end up with a squeaky voice and panting for breath. Relaxing

will help make your voice stronger, so try the pre-presentation relaxer on page 36.

You can make sure that you have got the volume right by asking, 'Can everyone hear me?' If the answer is 'no' make your voice twice as loud.

Remember your voice will sound much louder to you, as it resonates inside your head, than it will to your audience. So don't be afraid that you are booming away − it's very unlikely that you are.

Remember, if you're addressing an audience of more than a dozen people, you're not having a cosy chat with friends over a dinner party. Imagine being on a theatrical stage and rise to the occasion.

6 *Tricks to help you make a fluent speech*

Don't try to learn your speech off by heart; you're not in a stage play and it'll probably only sound false. By the same token, never, ever, read a speech − it rarely has the desired effect and your audience might wonder why they bothered coming.

Once you've written out your speech in full, transfer it to cards − slightly bigger than postcard size. Make sure your handwriting is legible! Then go through your speech over and over again until you are thoroughly familiar with every word and phrase. Work out where you're going to pause and which points you want to stress. Take a red or contrasting pen and underline these words. Practise making your speech out loud. You'll find that very soon you can make the speech by just glancing at your cards between sentences or even paragraphs. The effect of using this technique is to enable you to maintain all-important eye contact with your audience, without becoming desperately anxious as you try to remember what comes next. Your cards are your security blanket, don't leave home without them!

7 *Maintain eye contact*

We talked about the importance of eye contact earlier. It is never so vital as when you get up to give a talk or make a presentation. If you don't look at your audience you'll never know whether they're following you or if they've all walked out. Make your audience feel involved − look at them. You can't make contact with a hundred pairs of eyes, of course, so when you face an audience, fix on three or four points: one close to you, one each to the left and right and one way out at the back – even if you can't actually see the person. As you go through what you have to say, focus a sentence or two on each of your 'eye points'. Watch that you don't start swivelling your head like a mechanical toy.

8 Don't wobble around

There's nothing worse than a speaker who can't stand still, except one that twiddles her glasses off and on her nose or rattles money in her pocket. Don't attempt to speak balanced precariously on one leg; you'll fall over as soon as you stick one arm out to emphasise a crucial point. Give yourself confidence by getting a good stable base. Stand with your feet slightly apart, so that you feel firm. You should find that you can turn quite easily from side to side without unbalancing. If you're not worrying about overbalancing, you'll feel more secure and deliver a more assertive presentation. Keep your arms under control. By all means use them to emphasise what you want to say, but don't wave them around – you'll only distract your audience.

9 Keep your upper body free

If you put your hand over your face, no one will hear what you're saying. Help yourself to project your voice clearly by keeping your upper body open. This means no hunching or folded arms. If you scrunch up, you'll tense up and restrict your breathing; the result, squeaky breathlessness. For more on voice projection see pages 85–86.

10 Remember, the show must go on

Don't let a minor slip ruin your performance. While your blunder might go on ringing inside your head, the chances are your audience will have forgotten all about it within a split second – unless you draw their attention to it. If you mispronounce a word, make a Freudian slip or stumble over a sentence, put it right out of your mind and carry straight on. And if the worst does happen – your papers fall all over the floor, all your slides appear upside down or your wonderfully chunky beads snap and roll all over the podium, brush it off with humour or downright honesty, even in front of the sternest of audiences. With a smile on your face, try saying something like, *'Is this room spooked?'* *'Well, it's just not my morning'*, *'I dreaded this – they say it happens to even the best speakers...'*, *'Well, we seem to have something of a technical error, if you'll just bear with me for a moment...'*

11 Keep them hanging on for more
Rather make a presentation that's too short than one that's too long. For this reason, you should always time what you have to say – especially if you've only two or three minutes in which to say it. Remember, the shorter your speech, the fewer the points you can put over. Unless you are giving an academic lecture, never speak for more than about forty minutes or your audience will lose concentration. If it's appropriate, leave plenty of time for questions.

12 Get the technical know-how
If you're using any kind of technical equipment always ensure that first, it's working properly and second, you know how to operate it! If you're using a microphone, always test it before you begin. You can do this by saying something like, *'Good Morning'* or *'Ladies and Gentlemen...'*. If you aren't happy with the angle or height, don't proceed until you've had it adjusted. If the microphone is fixed, remember not to move away otherwise your audience will lose what you're saying. The microphone isn't an ice cream so don't attempt to eat it. Don't bellow into it either; speak a fraction more strongly, rather than loudly, than you usually do.

POSITIVE INTERVIEWS

Attending a job interview is like scaling the penultimate peak of a mountain. You sense the success of having climbed this far, your ultimate goal is within your grasp but you haven't grabbed it yet.

Think how much creative and nervous energy goes into applying for a new job. Is it the right move? Does the work sound exciting? Have you got the qualifications? What about the pay and conditions, will you gain or will you make sacrifices? What's the competition going to be like? And then there are all the other pressures – family, money, responsibilities, the drive to move onwards and upwards, to make a change, to get out of a rut. And what if you have no choice, you're out of a job, this is your three-hundredth application and you're feeling at your lowest ebb?

If you're relaxed, enthusiastic and well prepared it's obvious that the interview will be more positive – and more successful – than if you enter the room with a mournful expression and the conviction that the whole process is a waste of time. Like any other situation where the stakes are high, where you've got a limited amount of time to make an impression, preparation is the key. You need to look the part and think the part. To make other people believe in you, you've got to believe in yourself. Before you go along to an interview, give your self-esteem a good old stoke up. Make a list of everything you're good at, spend time choosing your clothes and applying your make-up, walk tall down the street. Have a look at pages 26–36, Assertive Body Talk, and also at Chapter 7, Looking Good, Feeling Good, for more tips and advice. Set out convinced you're going to wow them! Make a Rights Charter for job-hunting:

- I have the right to be pleased with myself for gaining an interview.
- I have the right to promote my skills.
- I have the right to be respected as a serious candidate.
- I have the right to feel disappointed if I don't get the job.
- I have the right to try again somewhere else.
- I have the right to believe I will succeed.

And study the top tips overleaf.

Top tips for job interviews

1 *Prepare*

The more prepared you are the more confident you will be, and the less there will be to worry about. Find out as much as you can about the job and the company before you go. Look back over the original advertisement and your CV or application form. Make a list of all the skills and qualities the company are looking for and how you can fulfil them. Do some research on the company's products or services. Find out what else is going on in that particular market. Look through the relevant trade magazines to see what's hot news. Even if you're just starting out on the career ladder or you're going for a basic grade job, it's worth finding out what you can about your prospective employer. The more you know, the more in control you will feel.

Try to find out how the interview will be conducted; who your interviewer will be, whether there will be a panel of people and if you'll have to complete any tests. Think through the sort of questions you might be asked. Prepare answers, especially to the sticky ones, like 'I see from your CV that you've failed every maths exam you've ever taken; why do you think you'd make a good bookkeeper?' If you've thought about everything they could possibly ask you at the interview you won't sit there worrying what the next question is going to be and how you're going to answer it. Your performance will be more relaxed and professional.

One other vital preparation is to make sure you've planned how you're going to get to the interview – on time! Never, never be late.

2 *Be nice to everyone*

From the moment you enter the building until the second you leave, be nice to everyone, from the porter, the receptionist and the secretary to the managing director. Smile, say good morning or afternoon, thank them. Let them think what a friendly, polite person you are, the sort of colleague they'd like to have around. Don't forget that your interviewer may well ask colleagues for their impressions of you. Every good influence helps. By being friendly and smiling you'll have helped yourself to feel good inside and be in a bright and responsive frame of mind.

3 *Sell yourself*

Think of yourself as a vacuum cleaner or a washing machine that you're selling to a customer. If you don't put over your good points and tell the interviewer how suited you are for the job, then who will? Tell the company what you can do for them – dynamic senior managers and efficient secretaries add equally to the success of the company.

If you've been out of the job market for a while, perhaps to raise children, it can be difficult to match child rearing and household duties to executive positions. Think about your role as mother and housekeeper and any responsibilities you've taken on a voluntary basis. Organisational and communication skills are important whether you've picked them up at home, your local playgroup or your church. Make these experiences work for you, use them positively to boost your chance of getting the job you want. Believe in yourself, your abilities and their value. You can't possibly convince others of your worth if you don't believe in it yourself. If you believe in your ability to do the job in question, you will be able to sell yourself to the interviewer assertively.

4 *Be enthusiastic*

Be enthusiastic about the job on offer. Show your interviewer that you really want it and that you're interested in the company. Whatever else you do, don't gush. On the whole, less is more in a job interview. Answer questions with enthusiasm but keep your responses short, don't ramble. If you're asked about your family, you could answer for example, '*I'm married and I've got three teenage sons*'. On no account embark on a long-winded story about what each of them wants to do, how they've got girlfriend troubles and how one of them failed his last biology exam.

5 *Ask intelligent questions*

The aim of the interview is not just to give the company the chance to give you the once over, it's your opportunity to find out something about your potential employers. Many people find that, having got to the interview, they discover that they don't actually relish the prospect of a job with that particular company. It may be that you don't like the answers to the questions you ask or you're not keen on their attitude. Prepare two or three intelligent questions – ask for more information about an aspect of the job or the company, find out from your interviewer how they think the company will develop. By all means ask about pay, holidays and working conditions, but keep that right until the end and make it extremely brief.

6 *Dress appropriately*
In job interviews first impressions count. Wear something that is appropriate to the position and job you're after. Boost your confidence by selecting an outfit that you know you look really good in. And make sure you feel comfortable – you don't want to sit there dying to take your shoes off or fiddling with your bra strap. Have a look at the tips in Chapter 7, pages 163–174.

7 *Maintain eye contact*
Try to keep your hair off your face and don't put your hand up in front of your mouth. Smile – don't grin – and maintain eye contact. See pages 29–30.

While we're on the subject of what to do with bits of your anatomy, when you're invited to sit down, don't slop around. Sit up straight and tidily in your chair. Have your CV and a pen and paper to hand. If you're offered a coffee and you can't see anywhere to put it and you feel flustered and nervous, decline with an assertive, 'no thank you'.

8 *Don't outstay your welcome*
Be aware of the close of interview signals – ignore them at your peril. Usually the interviewer will say something like, 'Do you have any further questions?' or 'Thank you for coming today', or perhaps lean back and look at the clock. At this stage, don't try to prolong the interview. When you get the message that the interview is over, you could say something like, '*Thank you for taking the time to see me. The interview was very interesting and I'd very much like to do the job.*' Don't forget to finish with a good assertive handshake.

If you leave anything in the room, don't go back for it, ask a secretary or receptionist to fetch it for you.

9 *Follow up*

After the interview make a note of the name of the person or people who interviewed you, what they asked and what you thought of the job and the company. This is particularly important if you've been chasing a number of vacancies. If you still want the job, send your interviewer a brief letter of thanks. Say you enjoyed meeting them and learning about the company, that the interview confirmed your interest in the job and that it's one you feel you could do well. Keep the letter to three or four lines at most. This way you help yourself to stand out from the crowd.

5

The Assertion
Quiz

This is your chance to discover how far you've travelled along
the road to assertion. Can you recognise assertive and non-
assertive behaviour? Test yourself with this questionnaire. Three
different responses are given for each situation. Tick whether
you think the response is aggressive, non-assertive (passive or
manipulative) or assertive. Since there are no 'stage directions',
you'll have to imagine how each response might be conveyed —
the tone of voice, inflections and gestures. Remember, the
way you say something is just as important as the words you
use.

Situation 1

You've made a special dinner for close friends. They finally turn
up an hour and a half late without having phoned to say they've
been delayed at work. You say:

A *Hi. Come in, dinner's all ready.*

assertive   aggressive   non-assertive

B *Why the hell didn't you phone me? This is the last time I'm inviting you to dinner.*

assertive   aggressive   non-assertive

C *I've been waiting an hour and a half. I would have appreciated you phoning to let me know you'd be late.*

assertive   aggressive   non-assertive

Situation 2

You're sitting in a reception area with a no smoking sign. Someone sits down next to you and lights up. You say:

A *What on earth do you think you're doing? Can't you see there's a no smoking sign? Put that filthy cigarette out immediately.*

assertive   aggressive   non-assertive

B *Why do I always end up next to the smoker?*

assertive   aggressive   non-assertive

C *This is a no smoking area. Please would you put your cigarette out.*

assertive   aggressive   non-assertive

Situation 3

A friend compliments you on what you're wearing. It's new and you really like it. You say:

A *Thanks. I'm glad you like it.*

assertive   aggressive   non-assertive

B *Oh ... um ... I got it cheap ... um ...*

assertive   aggressive   non-assertive

C *This old thing? It's nothing special.*

assertive   aggressive   non-assertive

Situation 4

A colleague has just criticised a friend. You feel the criticism is unjustified. You say:

A *Perhaps you're right.*

assertive   aggressive   non-assertive

B *Oh shut up. You're not so perfect yourself.*

assertive   aggressive   non-assertive

C *I think what you've just said is unfair. I've never known her to behave like that.*

assertive   aggressive   non-assertive

Situation 5

You're going out with a group of friends and you're all deciding where to eat. Someone has just suggested a restaurant you don't like. You say:

A *I'm not that keen, but I suppose if you want to go...*

assertive   aggressive   non-assertive

B *You're so selfish, you always choose places you want to go to. Why don't you ever consider other people?*

assertive   aggressive   non-assertive

C *I really don't like that restaurant. How about the new one on the High Street?*

assertive   aggressive   non-assertive

Situation 6

Your parents telephone you to say that they're coming to visit for the weekend. You were looking forward to a quiet couple of days. You say:

A *Fine, when will you be arriving?*

assertive   aggressive   non-assertive

B *Not this weekend. I plan to have a couple of days off.*

assertive   aggressive   non-assertive

C *What again? You can't expect me to drop all my plans just for you, I've got my own life to lead.*

assertive   aggressive   non-assertive

Situation 7

Someone new moves into your road. You see her in the supermarket. Do you:

A Give her a wide berth and hide in the next aisle?

assertive   aggressive   non-assertive

B Smile vaguely and walk by?

assertive   aggressive   non-assertive

C Go up to her and say, '*Hi, I'm... I live over the road from you. I'm really glad to meet you. How are things going?*'

assertive   aggressive   non-assertive

Situation 8

You've just returned from a holiday with someone you love, you've had a great time and you want to tell them so. You say:

A *I really love you. Thank you for a great holiday.*

assertive   aggressive   non-assertive

B *The holiday wasn't bad, was it?*

assertive   aggressive   non-assertive

C *Let's see how much post has piled up.*

assertive   aggressive   non-assertive

Situation 9

You're up to your eyes with work. Your colleague comes in and asks you to do some of his jobs so that he can get away on time. You say:

A *Forget it. Do it yourself. I'm up to my eyes without your work.*

assertive   aggressive   non-assertive

B *I'm a bit busy. But all right, give it to me.*

assertive   aggressive   non-assertive

C *No. I'm up to my eyes, I'm not prepared to take on your work. I'd also like to leave on time.*

assertive   aggressive   non-assertive

Situation 10

Your small child is running around your living-room, despite being told not to, and knocks a valuable vase on to the floor. You say:

A *Oh, never mind.*

assertive   aggressive   non-assertive

B *You stupid, clumsy child. I told you not to run around, now look what you've done, you idiot.*

assertive   aggressive   non-assertive

C *I'm very cross that you disobeyed me. I asked you not to run around. You've knocked that valuable vase on the floor and broken it, which was clumsy.*

assertive   aggressive   non-assertive

How well have you done?

Situation 1

A = non-assertive: You pretend that nothing has happened and carry on as if your friends' behaviour is acceptable.
B = aggressive: You react like a cat in a temper and threaten your friends.
C = assertive: You tell your friends that they are late and offer constructive criticism.

Situation 2

A = aggressive: Very dogmatic and judgemental, guaranteed to put the smoker's back up.

B = non-assertive: Martyr syndrome, 'why me?', but you do nothing to remedy the situation.

C = assertive: Your request is clear and straightforward.

Situation 3

A = assertive: You accept and acknowledge the compliment.

B = non-assertive: You don't accept the compliment.

C = non-assertive: You deny the compliment even though deep down you agree with it.

Situation 4

A = non-assertive: Although you don't actually agree with your colleague, your response implies that you do.

B = aggressive: You become very hostile and put down your colleague.

C = assertive: You express how you feel and reject what you consider is invalid criticism.

Situation 5

A = non-assertive: You don't express your opinion openly, but suggest that you're prepared to go along with the crowd even though you really don't want to.

B = aggressive: You attack your friend with a put down, 'you're so selfish', and don't offer another suggestion.

C = assertive: You express how you feel and suggest an alternative choice.

Situation 6

A = non-assertive: You don't really want your parents to come down but you imply that it's okay if they do. You don't express how you feel or what you had intended to do.

B = assertive: You're upfront. You tell your parents you have other plans.

C = aggressive: You put your parents down, implying they make too many demands on you but without expressing how you feel about their last-minute call.

Situation 7

A = non-assertive: Avoidance techniques are not assertive! What have you to lose by simply making contact?
B = non-assertive: Smiling is good nonverbal behaviour but if it's just the merest hint of upturned lips and isn't followed by any kind of verbal communication then it's definitely non-assertive in this situation.
C = assertive: You go up and introduce yourself in a friendly way.

Situation 8

A = assertive: You express your feelings directly and offer a compliment.
B = non-assertive: You don't express your true feelings and hedge around the issue sending out confused messages.
C = non-assertive: Again you don't express your feelings and avoid the subject altogether.

Situation 9

A = aggressive: You don't say how you feel about your colleague's demands and answer very abruptly, sending out very confused signals.
B = non-assertive: You don't acknowledge to your colleague how you really feel and take on the work even though you haven't the time to do it. How many times will this happen again?
C = assertive: You give a very clear response – you also have every right to get away on time.

Situation 10

A = non-aggressive: You do mind about the broken vase but you carry on as if you didn't.
B = aggressive: You indulge in destructive name-calling.
C = assertive: You express your feelings and offer constructive criticism.

Give yourself one point for every correct answer. There's a top score of thirty points. How well did you do?

If you scored 25 or more, you're well on the way to becoming assertive. Read on! If you scored less than 25, why not check back over some of the earlier chapters to refresh your memory.

6

Assertive Solutions to Everyday Situations

In this part of the book we look at a range of everyday situations that crop up in the family or with friends, at work or in the high street, consider some of the issues that they raise and explore how you can deal with them assertively.

For each situation there is an Assertive Solution, a practical, logical way to tackle the problem. This is split into five straightforward steps:

Step One: Face the Facts, is about putting all your cards on the table, exploring what the situation's really about and confronting how you feel.
Step Two: My Options, looks at all the choices you could make to deal with the situation.
Step Three: Take the Challenge, considers the consequences of taking up each of your Step Two options.
Step Four: Make a Choice, is about doing precisely that!
Step Five: Make a Gameplan, is about thinking through how you're going to put your assertive solution into assertive action. It brings together the skills we've looked at in other parts of the book, particularly writing a survival script.

You might identify strongly with the people featured in these situations, or they may only reflect a passing resemblance to your own family, friends or colleagues. Don't take them literally, look for parallels and similarities with your own life, for they tackle common down-to-earth issues that confront very many women in one form or another. Use the Assertive Solution format to approach other situations which you find difficult to handle or which bother you.

LEAD YOUR OWN LIFE

Susie: *My mother is driving me mad. She keeps interfering in and criticising everything I do. I'm single, she thinks I should be married and keeps trying to fix me up with what she thinks are eligible men. I work part time in a shop so that I can spend the rest of my days being creative. I make pots and paint them and I'm beginning to build up a small business selling them to local gift shops. My mother thinks this is a waste of time and I should get myself a 'proper job'. She rings me every day, complaining about one thing or another. I know she's been through a rough time, my father died recently and she took it very badly. All the same, whenever she telephones, I can feel myself making an excuse to finish the call quickly. She's talking about the two of us going away on holiday together. I don't know whether I could handle it. I love her dearly but I wish she'd leave me alone.*

There must be millions of people living their lives according to someone else's ambitions and desires. Working at jobs they hate, living in houses they abhor, socialising with people they despise, marrying spouses they don't really love. Many more shut their ears and bite their tongues while busybodies try to map out their careers for them.

It can be a struggle to be yourself. We get so many messages telling us what to do, where to go, what to say. Parents devise glorious schemes for their unborn children. Little Georgie will ride out the failures of generations past and go on to be one of the great and the good. And we get parental prejudices — what was good enough for us is good enough for young Mary. Peer groups, schools, advertisers imprint on us images of the sort of lives we ought to lead. Empowering people to make their own decisions is certainly important. Counselling, listening, guiding, advising all have a place. But trying to dictate someone else's life for them doesn't. The problem is, the person who's doing the dictating is often someone who's close to you, who, much as you may feel bitter towards them or frustrated by their interference, you still don't want to hurt. It can be very hard to change the pattern of many years. But can you afford the price if you don't?

No two people are the same. Only you can really know what it is you want and how you want it. If you live according to someone else's plan, who will guide you when they're no longer there? By then you may think it too late to strike out on your own. Set your own goals, carve your own path, be brave enough to live only your own life. This is Susie's assertive solution:

Step one: face the facts

- My mother is an opinionated woman. She has always been very critical of me and I've never confronted her about this.
- Her criticisms undermine my self-confidence and make me wonder whether I'm doing the right thing.
- I enjoy being single. I haven't ruled out marriage, but only if and when I find the right person. I resent my mother implying that my single status is less satisfactory than being married.
- I'm a good potter and artist. I'm optimistic that my business will take off.
- My mother has been badly affected by my father's death. I'm all she has now. I feel responsible towards her.
- Even though, on the whole, I like my mother's company, I don't think a fortnight away would work out.

Step two: my options

- I could say nothing and agree to go away together.
- I could explain how I feel, ask her to stop criticising me and refuse to go away.

- I could offer to go away for a weekend to see how things work out.

Step three: take the challenge

- If I say nothing, I'll resent my mother even more, have less to do with her and feel guilty because I'll think I'm being mean. If we go away, it'll be a disaster!
- If I get my frustrations out into the open, I'll feel better. She'll probably be really taken aback, she won't expect a tough response from me. If I refuse to go away altogether, I think she'll be upset and then I'll feel really bad. But she'd get over it, so I shouldn't feel guilty. Perhaps if I've talked to her, a holiday won't be so bad – for a week.

Step four: make a choice

- I'm satisfied with the way I'm living my life and I think I've got the right to live the way I want to without my mother interfering. I am going to tell her how I feel and ask her to stop criticising my job and the fact that I'm single. I am not going to make a decision about the holiday until I feel comfortable about our relationship. I acknowledge that my mother is going through a rough time. I think I am being helpful and supportive. I will not feel guilty if I choose not to go away with her.

Step five: make a gameplan

Susie decides to invite her mother round to tea so she can talk to her face to face. She also thinks about taking her mother round some of the local shops that are selling her painted pots. Susie then works out what she is going to say to her mother and gets some responses ready to what she knows will be her mother's stock set of criticisms.

Susie: *I know I've never been direct with you before and I imagine you might be taken aback by what I have to say. I feel very hurt and resentful about how you criticise the way I live my life − the fact that I am single and the work I do. I enjoy being single and I have chosen to do part time work so that I can use my artistic talents. My business looks as if it's doing very well. I'd like to have your support. I know you have strong opinions and I'd welcome positive comments and ideas you may have, but please don't make negative criticisms. I don't intend to change the way I do things. I don't think that going away for a fortnight's holiday would be a good idea at the moment. Perhaps we can see how things work out and then we can discuss going away for a weekend.*

Susie's mum: *I know you like playing around with clay and paints but it's not a proper job. You never know where your next pay packet's coming from. You're wasting your brain.*

Susie: *I know you don't think what I do is a proper job but it's what I've chosen to do. I enjoy it and I think I can make it pay. In the meantime my shop work brings in enough money to pay the rent. I'm using my creative skills and that's what matters to me. I would welcome your support and some positive comments. I am not going to change what I do.*

Susie's mum: *Mark my words. This creative stuff never pays. You need security.*

Susie: *For the moment, my business is doing well and I enjoy it. If necessary I may rethink what I do, but certainly not for now. If and when I do, I'll discuss it with you.*

Susie's mum: *At your age you should be married. It's not right that you're still single. You know I'm trying to find someone for you to meet.*

Susie: *I know that you want me to find a husband but I find it very irritating when you keep introducing me to men you think are suitable. I am happy being single. If and when I meet someone, I may get married. Please let me deal with this my own way.*

Susie resolves that she will weather her mother's opinions and remind her mother of how she feels whenever she criticises her. Susie is sure in her own mind that she is doing the right thing with her life.

NEGOTIATE THE CHORE WAR

Carole: *My partner and I have got really demanding jobs. We leave early in the morning and I often don't get back until late evening. Mark's a fitness fanatic and he tends to go to the gym after work. Despite the fact that we both work long hours, I'm the one who has to deal with all the household chores – organising the cleaning, the washing, shopping and so on. At weekends Mark tends to either slop around or if I suggest he does some clearing up, then he disappears off to the gym. He says I'm just too fussy about the flat and all I do is nag him when he wants to relax. I'm beginning to really resent him and almost think I'd be better off living by myself.*

Money is the biggest source of partnership tensions, who does the clearing up is the second. Sounds crazy, but the two are often interlinked. Money is power and the person who has less power tends to clean the toilet. Unfortunately in most households, it's often the woman who earns less and that, coupled with the fact that domestic chores are traditionally seen as 'woman's work', means cleaning up is a job for the girls.

Even in the most liberated households the cleaning and the clearing remain top of the disagreement agenda. There are plenty of men who know where the vacuum cleaner lives and how to operate the washing machine. The problem is that they suppress their usual commando instincts and turn rank and file soldiers awaiting instructions from on high. The familiar cry, 'Just tell me what to clean/shop for/wash, darling, and I'll go and do it,' leaves thousands of men feeling virtuous and similar numbers of female hackles rising. What ever happened to joint responsibility and manly initiative?

107

Some of the blame must surely go on mothers who like the good fairy magicked every festering pile of dirty socks and unwashed plates into invisible suds and put squeaky clean or nicely folded ones back in their place. Their adolescents are the ones who grow up to complain that their mothers, unlike their female partners with their incessant nagging, were never half so fussy about dust and dirt. Small wonder, it was zapped before it ever hit the ground. The magic has worn a little thin these days. With more women out working and combining childcare and eldercare responsibilities, the chore war becomes increasingly pressurised. There are plenty of gadgets, dishwashers, washing machines and services like domestic cleaners and ironers to take away the aggro. But women simply cannot do everything. Superwoman, as we said early on, is not assertive.

Some people aren't bothered by unwashed clothes, plates and floors, so, if the whole family are in cahoots, why worry what others think? But if it's a source of constant aggravation, you need to tackle it head on − there is no known cure for dirt and mayhem. Here's Carole's assertive solution:

Step one: face the facts

- I resent the fact that the domestic chores end up as my responsibility. I think that Mark is being incredibly selfish not sharing these tasks.
- I think that my job is just as important to me as Mark's is to him. I feel he undervalues what I do.
- I feel frustrated. I'm in control of my life at work but I can't seem to manage something as simple as sorting out domestic responsibilities at home.
- I cannot live in a dirty, untidy home.
- I'm concerned about the future. I wonder what he will be like if we have children. Will I be the one left holding the baby? I don't think I could live with someone who was so unsupportive.
- I haven't really attempted to tackle this issue. I usually just sulk and we end up rowing in bed.

Step two: my options

- I could carry on as we are and hope things get better.
- I can explain how I feel to Mark and suggest some practical solutions.
- I can end the relationship before it gets more involved.

Step three: take the challenge

- If I do nothing, I don't think the situation will change. In fact I think the relationship will deteriorate. Mark will spend less time at home to avoid arguments and I'll spend less time at home to avoid clearing up. I think I'll feel even more out of control if we then break up.
- If I attempt to talk to Mark, he may just ignore me and go off to the gym. I might lose my temper or not speak to him for days, in which case we'll be back where we started. Alternatively he may be prepared to accept some practical suggestions that don't involve him in too many chores. I realise I will have to take the initiative in putting these into action.
- If Mark isn't prepared to listen and accept what I have to say then I can explain my long-term fears and say that I want to end our relationship. This might make him face the facts and change his attitude. If not I have to be prepared to carry out what I've said. It's going to be hard breaking up.

Step four: make a choice

- I'm not prepared to go on shouldering the responsibility for the household. I love Mark but unless he's willing to change his attitude, I cannot accept that we have a long-term future together. I will confront him about his behaviour and suggest some practical solutions to the problem. I will also tell him how I feel about the future. If he refuses to acknowledge what I have to say, or if our arrangements don't work out, then although it will be hard, I will end our relationship and move out.

Step five: make a gameplan

Carole decides that she needs to think of some practical solutions to her domestic crises and then consider how she is going to approach Mark.

These are Carole's practical solutions: *'We can afford to get someone in to clean and do the ironing once a fortnight. Any cleaning, washing or ironing in the meantime is our own responsibility. I'm prepared to cook, if Mark does the washing up. We'll do the shopping together on a Thursday night — I'll pick Mark up directly from work.'* Carole then scripts what she is going to say to Mark. She decides that since Mark is more likely to walk out of the discussion than she is likely to lose her temper, she'll bring the matter up while they're out at a restaurant.

> Carole: *I imagine that you're not going to like what I'm going to say, but I feel it's affecting our relationship. It's about running the household. I'm angry that I'm left with the responsibility for organising the cleaning, washing, shopping and doing the cooking. We both work equally long hours at equally demanding jobs. I resent the fact that you go to the gym practically every evening and you disappear off at weekends when I suggest you might help me in the flat. I'd like you to respect that I can't live in a dirty flat and that since we both make the mess, we should both clear it up. I'm not prepared to continue as we are so I've thought of some practical solutions...*

Carole also imagines some of Mark's responses and scripts appropriate replies.

> Mark: *Why do you have to bring up this old story when we're out eating? Cleaning the flat is very boring. I work hard, I want to relax, I can't be bothered.*
> Carole: *I'm discussing this now, because I'm not prepared to let things continue as they are. I know you work hard and want to relax but I also work hard and I want to relax. I feel you're being very selfish putting your needs*

first, when our jobs are equally demanding. Yes, cleaning and shopping are very boring but I'm not prepared to live in a pig-sty and we have to eat. That's why I've made some suggestions that will involve both of us in the minimum of effort.

Mark: *If you're so fussed about the flat being tidy, then you deal with it. I'm fed up with all your nagging. I work hard, I deserve to relax. Now let's get on with our meal.*

Carole: *I'm not prepared to forget it. I don't think I'm being fussy. I'm just not willing to live in a pig-sty and neither am I willing to shoulder all the responsibility for cleaning and cooking. Much as I care for you now, I cannot see any future in our relationship if you're not prepared to acknowledge my feelings on this issue.*

Carole thinks that Mark may tell her she's over-dramatising the situation, that they're not going to split up over the washing-up and so on. Carole decides she'll stick to three things: that she wants Mark to acknowledge how she feels; that she's not prepared to go on as they have been doing and she wants them both to share the household responsibilities; that at the end of the day she wants a supportive partner who she feels treats her as an equal. Carole doesn't want to end the relationship but knows deep down that if Mark doesn't change his views they're unlikely to have a successful long-term future together.

UNTANGLE FAMILY TIES

Isabelle: *It's always been a family tradition that my husband and I take our two kids to spend Sunday with Tony's parents. We used to quite enjoy it. His mum's a good cook and they live in the country, so Tim and Sally have plenty of room to play. However, now the kids are getting older and I've gone back to work, we've got more demands on our time and quite honestly our weekly visits are becoming a bit of a chore. Tony's sister doesn't get on with her parents, so they don't see her and I know they feel very bitter about this. I don't want to upset them further or get cast in the wicked daughter-in-law role, but I'm beginning to dread the weekends.*

This must be a familiar cry the length and breadth of the country, not just at weekends but on high days and holy days too. Christmas is the ultimate nightmare. Only so many people can be accommodated round the festive turkey, Great-aunt Maud can't travel very far, the in-laws don't get on, should little Johnny open his stocking with mummy or with daddy? Families go to elaborate lengths not to offend one party or another. If it was Scunthorpe last year, it must be Little Snoring this. The result — exhausted people tearing up and down motorways before they've had a chance to digest their mince pies.

Tradition is an insidious thing. You do something three Sundays running and lo and behold, it's immovable. Tradition has set in. What were once pleasurable activities become duties. Other things take precedence in your life, but still the tradition continues. Starting up the car to visit your brother Jack on a Saturday afternoon sets off a bout of family bickering. As soon as you get to Jack's house, you look at your watch to see if it's time to go. Does anyone stop to count the cost in terms of excessive stress and soured relationships?

And when you break with tradition, there's always someone to moan that, 'things are no longer what they once were'. But families move on. Children grow into young adults and 'do their own thing'; individuals travel vast distances. The telephone becomes the main source of contact. And as relationships and family structures become increasingly complex, old notions of familial traditions are no longer applicable. With a growing elderly population, the burden of caring and maintaining contact will fall on younger (but not necessarily young) family members, the majority of whom will be women. The problem of reconciling the needs of the family, especially those who are dependent on you, with your own needs, isn't easy and takes courage. Here's Isabelle's assertive solution:

Step one: face the facts

- I like my parents-in-law very much, but the strain of having to see them every weekend is souring my view of them. I find myself making nasty comments about them which are completely unfounded.
- I'm feeling very stressed because I don't have enough time at the weekends to do the things I need to do. I think Tony feels the same way.
- My parents-in-law and I have always got on. Tony's their favourite son. I don't want to lose their approval.
- I've never told my parents-in-law how I feel. I'm just building up resentment. I don't know how they would react.
- I quite enjoy visiting them. At least I don't have to cook lunch!

Step two: my options

- I can keep quiet and not say anything and continue our weekly visits. The kids will eventually want to stay at home on Sundays, so I could wait a couple of years until then.
- I can talk to them about how I feel and suggest a compromise, that we go once every four weeks.

Step three: take the challenge

- If I say nothing, and try and pack everything into a short weekend, I'm just going to get more uptight.
- If I say something, then they might get upset, no matter how reasonable my suggestion. They might try to make us feel guilty over Tony's sister. They might be less friendly towards me.

Step four: make a choice

- I'm not prepared to continue with the weekly visits. I have the right to have time for myself. I understand that my parents-in-law feel bitter about Tony's sister, but her behaviour is not my responsibility. I will live with the fact that they may be less approving of me initially but I don't think this attitude will last. This is something that Tony and I must approach together.

Step five: make a gameplan

Isabelle decides she needs to tackle two things. '*1. I must talk to Tony first, so that we both agree. 2. I must prepare what I will say to my parents-in-law.*' She knows that Tony has been moaning about the weekly visits, so it's important to get him to acknowledge his feelings too. If they speak with one voice, they stand a better chance of getting his parents to accept what they are suggesting. Isabelle explains to Tony how she feels and asks him what his thoughts are. She suggests the compromise of visiting once a month, which Tony thinks is a good idea.

She then thinks through what she will say to her parents-in-law on the next visit.

I know how much you look forward to our Sunday visits — I certainly appreciate the chance to enjoy a Sunday lunch I don't have to cook! But since I've gone back to work and the kids have got older, we've had a lot more demands on our time. I'm finding it very hard to fit everything into the weekend — and keep my sanity. We'd like to continue to come down to see you regularly, but we want to come once a month instead of every week. I imagine you'll be disappointed but I'm sure both Tony and I will be better company once we've been able to relax a bit more.

Isabelle also considers some of the responses she might get and how she will reply.

Tony's parents: *You and Tony's sister are all alike. No one's interested in us — you're all too busy to care. We'll end up losing contact with all our family.*

Isabelle: *I don't think what you have just said is true.*

114

We've always kept in contact with you and we'll continue to do so. The only difference is we'll come once a month instead of every week. We care for you just as much, but I need some time at the weekends for myself and my other commitments.

Tony's parents: *If you stay at home you'll just rush around. It's much more relaxing here. Tony's mum enjoys cooking lunch — who's she going to cook for now?*

Isabelle: *If we have more time at home each weekend we won't have to rush around. That means we can really relax here when we come. I imagine it will be a let-down not being able to cook for us each Sunday, but perhaps you can prepare something special for when we do visit. We'll look forward to it.*

Isabelle decides that whatever happens, she will stick to her guns. The weekly visits are a thing of the past!

DEAL WITH TEENAGE TRAUMAS

Judy: *My daughter's fourteen and has just woken up to the wild delights of being a teenager. She's discovered make-up, loud music, boys and late parties. My husband, Derek, has been taking a tough line. I think part of him still thinks Chloe's a little child while the other imagines her being enticed into a late night orgy of drink and drugs. As a result we've had nothing but rows, door slamming and sulks for the last couple of months. As usual I find myself in the middle. I want to let Chloe grow up and have some freedom, I think she's pretty level headed. At the same time she is only fourteen and she's got her school work to think about. How on earth can I keep the peace?*

Nearly every family has a peacemaker. Whether it's mum or dad, brother, sister, granny, aunt or nanny, most of the family run in the same direction when things don't work out. Diplomat and confidante, one person sorts out the squabbles. Playing Solomon can be a bit of a burden. You do your best but somehow you can never win — especially if you're piggy in the middle and one of the opponents is a teenager!

Much has been said and written about the terrible teens — the angst and the acne. But the dilemmas teenagers face as they seek their independent way in the adult world are ones which many people face in different forms throughout their lives, whether it's the toddler striking out on her first few unsteady words and steps or the middle-aged man or woman coming to terms with a 'mid-life crisis'. It's hard not to be judgemental from the lofty heights of forty or fifty years of experience of the universe. You may recall your own teenage years with anguish as you sense again the frustration, inadequacy or embarrassment you felt. By the same token you may look back on those years and remember nothing but sunshine and driving ambition. Perhaps you feel you've lost those qualities or want your child to recapture what you once had. Remember, each generation and each individual has its own goals, its own dilemmas, its own pressures. Examine your own experiences and prejudices before you apply them to your offspring.

The teenage years, by definition, are more than likely to be unsettling. One moment you've got a cocksure rebel on your hands clamouring to be treated like an adult, resenting and resisting all forms of parental constraint; the next minute, the rebel has dissolved into a baby pool of uncertainty, demanding reassurance and support. Some conflict is inevitable. Teenagers, like toddlers, need to know where they stand. They want the security of clearly defined limits. They need something solid to rebel against, something that won't disintegrate no matter how hard they beat their fists.

Patience may be a virtue but it's also a fairly elusive quality when you're at your wits' end. However patience is what's called for, along with tolerance, an abundance of love, a willingness to listen, to talk, to be available and not to jump to conclusions. Anyone with teenagers in tow has to strike a balance between enabling them to bid effectively for independence while providing a caring, stable base for them to return to when they need to recover from the hurt of their mistakes or to bolster their self-esteem.

Finally, learning to interact in the world can be a hard business whether you're an adult, a teenager or a child. Behaving assertively and having faith in yourself can go a long way to making the experience a lot more positive and productive – for everyone. Here's Judy's assertive solution:

Step one: face the facts

- I'm getting fed up with the arguments and the tension in the house.
- I resent playing peacemaker; it's all getting very tiring.
- I'm sure my daughter is responsible, but I worry about her getting into situations which she finds difficult to handle.
- Derek and I haven't really had a heart to heart about setting down the rules about boys, staying out late and so on. We're making the rules up as we go along, so Chloe doesn't really know where she stands – and nor do I.
- I remember feeling very confused and very awkward at her age. I'd rather she didn't have to go through what I did.

Step two: my options

- I can let things ride along as they are and keep my fingers crossed that it doesn't get too rough.
- I can confront both Derek and Chloe and tackle the issues head on.

Step three: take the challenge

- If I do nothing, they may well end up going at each other like cat and dog. That would make the house unbearable to live in. I think my relationship with Derek would deteriorate – none of this would do Chloe any good.

- If I tackle the issue, I expect there'll be a few initial explosions but I think we'll all have a better idea of what is and what isn't acceptable. At least we'll know what we're arguing about!

Step four: make a choice

- I'm not prepared to go on playing peacemaker — I've got the right to live a reasonably stress-free existence. Derek must trust Chloe more and realise that I'm not prepared to patch up after them. I think it's important to provide clear guide-lines for Chloe and that's something we should agree on together.

Step five: make a gameplan

Judy decides to concentrate on three things: '*1. I want to talk to Derek and ask him to trust Chloe more and I want to explain how I feel. 2. I want us to decide how we're going to tackle the boyfriend issue, staying out late and loud music. 3. I want to explain what the rules are to Chloe.*'

Judy decides to talk to Derek away from the house and certainly not while Chloe's around, so she suggests they go out for the evening on their own. She then scripts how she's going to broach the subject. She knows her husband well, so she also imagines how the conversation might develop.

Judy: *Over the last six months Chloe's really grown up. She's no longer a kid, she's become a young woman. I know she's going through all the usual teenage dilemmas, but I'm finding the arguments in the house are really getting me down. I'm fed up with keeping the peace between the two of you. I wish you'd trust her a bit more. I'd like us to come up with some reasonable rules about staying up late and playing her music instead of rocketing from one outburst to another.*

Derek: *It's hardly my fault, she just doesn't know how to behave. She needs a good firm hand.*

Judy: *Derek, she's a teenager. Come on, we were both*

pretty much the same when we were her age. Shouting at her's not going to achieve much.

Derek: *I was a boy, that's different. I'm not having a daughter of mine parading around with muck all over her face, out until all hours with a bunch of tearaways.*

Judy: *Hang on. Chloe doesn't stay out until all hours and her friends are basically a nice bunch of kids. I imagine you do worry but she's a responsible girl. What do you think goes on at these parties?*

Derek: *How do I know? Sex, alcohol, cigarettes, drugs.*

Judy: *Have you ever talked to Chloe? She doesn't smoke, she thinks drugs are stupid. She's not daft, why don't you trust her?*

Derek: *Well...*

Judy: *Look I agree with you, I think we should lay down some rules, let her know where we stand, but there's no point shouting about it. How about if we say she needs to be back by 9.30 on school days — providing she's done her homework — and by 11.00 at the weekends, and that we must know where she's going to be and how she's getting home.*

Derek: *All right, but what about boys and what about that dreadful music?*

Judy: *We can't stop her seeing boys — it's all part of growing up. She knows what we think about sex and sleeping around, as I said she's not stupid and she does respect us. As for the music, well whatever she does in her room is her own business so long as we can't hear it in the rest of the house.*

Derek: *Okay, I'll try and keep my temper.*

Judy: *Thanks. I really couldn't go on as we were.*

Judy reckons that she'll get Derek to see reason but she'll also have to talk to Chloe and persuade her that her dad's not the ogre she thinks he is. She decides to confront Chloe while Derek is out. Here's part of the script she drafts:

Judy: *I know you think your dad can be a bit of a tyrant but he means well, he's worried about you.*

Chloe: *Is he? I can take care of myself!*

Judy: *Yes I know you can, and yes he is anxious. I think he imagines that your parties are one long orgy of sex and drugs.*

Chloe: *That's stupid. Doesn't he trust me?*

Judy: *Well, we had a chat and I think he does now. But there are some things which we do think are important like what time you get home and how you get home.*

Chloe: *You're being neurotic.*

Judy: *No I'm not, you are still only just fourteen. School work matters and your safety matters.* (Judy outlines her 'rules' about staying out late) ... *And as for your music...*

Chloe: *Mum, don't be such a stick in the mud.*

Judy: *Maybe I am. I don't mind what you do in your room as long as the rest of the house doesn't have to hear it — we all have to live here.*

Judy realises that the next few years aren't going to be without their ups and downs but she resolves to stand firm, to ignore some of the mental bruises she's sure she'll suffer and to offer Chloe as much love and stability as she and Derek can give.

SAY 'NO' TO THE CROWD

Louise: *I'm going away with a group of people over the summer. I don't know most of the people — they're all friends of a good pal of mine called Wendy. I met them briefly the other week and now I'm having second thoughts about the whole thing. They seem a pretty rowdy bunch and they were talking about going water skiing and scuba diving and doing all sorts of things I'd be scared stiff of. I'd much rather read or go off and explore interesting places. Although I've been away with Wendy before and we both enjoyed ourselves, I think I might end up being the odd one out this time. Much as I'd like to go, I don't want them to think I'm a wet blanket and I don't want to end up wishing I'd stayed at home.*

As children and teenagers we spend an inordinate amount of time trying to fit in with the crowd. On the whole, kids don't like to be different — unless 'being different' is the in thing. We worry about whether we wear the 'right' clothes, like the 'right' music, know the 'right' dances, say the 'right' thing. The fear of being ostracised looms large in many an adolescent nightmare.

On the whole, the older you get, the less significant fitting in with the crowd becomes. Each of us finds our own niche. We tend to socialise with people who are very much like ourselves, whose company we feel comfortable with, the crowd business is not such an issue. Usually we know what the score is. We have a fair idea of what to wear, what to say and what not to say. But in unfamiliar situations, the old nightmares still rear their ugly heads. You go back to work after a child-rearing break to find your workmates — as you see it — younger, trendier and high-tech happy. Or you enter a party full of strangers and think, 'I should have read the *Financial Times* and taken off my tan tights before I came.'

We all like to know the rules of the crowd game but sometimes we simply don't want to play by them. Some years ago it was extremely difficult not to drink alcohol in a pub or at a party. Now the tables seem to have turned. Fashions are fickle things. If you're happy to stay ahead of the pack, all well and good. If the rules don't suit, state your own. Whatever you do, don't join in if you don't want to play the game, unless you've chosen to take the consequences or you're doing it on your own terms. Here is Louise's assertive solution:

Step one: face the facts

- It takes me time to get to know people. I'm not naturally gregarious. Perhaps I've been a little hasty in judging this new group.
- Wendy is a good friend. I've known her a long time. I feel comfortable in her company.
- I was a bit taken aback that she was friendly with these other people. This has made me feel less secure about our relationship. Maybe she's bored with my company.

- I'm not a risk taker. I'm often reluctant to give new things a try.
- I am looking forward to two weeks in the sun. I had imagined it would be like our previous holiday. Perhaps I haven't adjusted to the fact that this year will be different.
- I enjoy doing nothing on holiday except reading and a bit of exploring. I don't mind going off by myself.

Step two: my options

- I can cancel the holiday immediately.
- I can talk to Wendy, explain my concerns and then make a decision.
- I can go anyway and make the best of it − try new things and not be afraid to say what I do and don't want to do.

Step three: take the challenge

- If I cancel, I'll lose my deposit. I might also lose Wendy's friendship. She might think me a spoil-sport. I think she'd be right. I think I'd have this on my conscience all summer, the fact that I didn't face up to my fears and that I might have enjoyed it all along.
- If I talk to Wendy before making a decision, then at least I'll get a clearer picture − maybe she's relying on me going so that we can go off and do some of the things we usually do together. If I decide to cancel after all, I'll feel more in control of the situation and that I've made a rational choice.
- If I go along, I have to accept that I might not enjoy it. I can look on the bright side. I'll have two weeks in the sun and I think the resort will be quite interesting. I might meet other people there. This is going to be a challenge for me.

Step four: make a choice

- I'll talk to Wendy before I make a decision. I have the right to tell her that I feel uncomfortable. If I choose to go, I'm going to learn to take a few risks — including the fact that I might not enjoy myself as much as I had imagined. I'm going to practise saying 'no' and making my own demands. I have the right not to be bullied into doing anything I don't want to. I also have the right to enjoy my holiday and do the things I want to. I'm going to learn to give and take a bit more.

Step five: make a gameplan

Louise decides that she needs to tackle four things: '*1. I must script what I'm going to say to Wendy. 2. I need to organise myself, so that I can go off and do the things I want to do while I'm on holiday. 3. I want to practise saying "no". 4. I want to practise making my own demands.*'

Louise starts off by thinking about how she's going to approach Wendy. She decides to call her immediately and arrange to meet after work.

I feel a bit awkward telling you this — it's about our summer holiday. We've been friends for years and I really enjoy your company. I was looking forward to going away, we've always had great fun. The thing is, I was a bit taken aback when I met the holiday crowd. I imagined that they'd be very much like you and me but they seem really boisterous and sporty and I felt very uncomfortable. I know they're good friends of yours and I realise I've only met them briefly, I don't want to misjudge them. I'd appreciate it if you could tell me a bit more about them. What do they do, how did you meet them — are they really as rowdy as they seemed to me?!

Louise gives Wendy the chance to tell her more about the crowd. Wendy admits that they can be rowdy and intimidating for people that don't know them but they're basically a good-natured group. She also says that she likes their company because it gives her a chance to do things that she doesn't do with Louise. Louise carries on:

Thanks for telling me that. I know I'm not a risk-taker and all the talk of scuba diving and water skiing made me feel really uncomfortable. I'd much rather curl up with a good book or go off to see the sights. I don't want to feel the odd one out and I was anxious that you might just think that I was a wet blanket.

Wendy tells Louise that she knows she's not into sport and that she doesn't have to do anything she doesn't want to — but that she ought to have a go. She also says that she's looking forward to Louise coming away so that if the others get too rowdy they can escape to a quiet corner together. Louise feels reassured and decides she will go ahead with the holiday plans, so she continues with her gameplan.

Louise thinks she ought to be ready to amuse herself if she chooses not to go along with what the others decide to do. She therefore makes a plan to: buy a good selection of books; read up on the resort and places of interest; brush up on the language; and take her driving licence so she can hire a car if she wants to. The next stage is to practise saying 'no'. She first makes herself a personal Rights Charter.

- I have the right to say 'no' to doing things which make me feel uncomfortable.
- I have the right to take risks. To take credit for taking the risk. To fail and choose not to take it again.
- I have the right to say what I want to do and when and how I want to do it. I have the right to be respected for the choices I make.

Then she scripts a couple of scenarios.

The Group: *Come on Louise, we're going water skiing, you've got to come along, it's brilliant, you can't miss it.*

Louise: *No thanks, I prefer to stay by the pool and read. It's a good book, I've just got to the exciting bit. I'll see you later, enjoy yourselves.*

The Group: *We're chartering a boat to go scuba diving. It's really amazing — Louise you ought to come along.*

Louise: *Okay, thanks, I will. I'd enjoy coming out in the boat. I'm not sure about the scuba diving. If someone will teach me what to do, I'll see how I get on but I'll only go as far as I feel comfortable.*

Louise then thinks about taking the lead on what she wants to do.

I'm going to hire a car and go off exploring one or two of the towns nearby. I've made a plan of what we could see and there are some great places to stop for lunch. Who wants to come along?

Louise knows that Wendy will come, and if the others want to, fine; if not, they'll go off on their own.

Finally, Louise decides that the holiday will be all part of life's rich experiences. She hopes she'll come back having met new people, done new things and become more assertive.

Shape Up

Jan: *I've got a real weight problem. I've tried to shed a few pounds but without success. I enjoy eating and when I go on a diet I just get miserable and end up eating even more. I don't like being overweight, I feel a right frump. The problem is my friend Marie, who can stuff herself silly and remain as skinny as a bean pole. What's more she's into fitness and aerobics. Whenever she sees me she wastes no time telling me how fat I am. She keeps nagging me to go on a diet and take exercise but then she sits in front of me consuming vast quantities of cakes and biscuits until I join in. I usually go home feeling angry with her and totally disgusted with myself. We used to get on really well but one day soon I think I'm going to explode at her.*

Perhaps if we all came off a production line with the same shaped bodies, identical complexions, matching hair colour and similar amounts of cellulite, we'd all be better off. But then wouldn't life be boring? To some extent our personalities are our bodies, larger than life or elfin dynamos − or like most, somewhere in between.

If deep inside you think you're a blond bombshell waiting to escape a mouse-coloured existence or that your buxom curvaceousness − which others would kill for − is hiding the flat-chested lissom being that's really you, then a bottle of peroxide or the surgeon's knife should do the trick. The cosmetic wonders of modern society mean we have the means to change the physical attributes we were born with. So what's wrong with a tummy tuck here or a low light there? Nothing. It doesn't make you any less assertive. If it makes you feel good, then that's great. What does matter is chasing hopeless dreams that pots of paint and pills will never realise. If your nose job doesn't make you feel glamorous, attractive and an altogether interesting person, then perhaps it wasn't your nose that needed fixing in the first place.

Altering the way you look can be a great boost to confidence − a good hair cut that people comment on, a new dress that makes you feel a million dollars. Gaining a few more pounds or losing a stone may make you fitter and healthier and do wonders for your self-esteem. Diets, beauty treatments, clothes and cosmetics are there to enhance you, not to recreate the very essence of you. Learn to love what you've got, then if you like, take advantage of what's on the market to get yourself into a shape you love even more. Here is Jan's assertive solution:

Step one: face the facts

- My weight is my crumple zone. I'm over-sensitive to comments about the way I look.
- I don't like being overweight. I don't feel comfortable. When I'm really overweight my behaviour changes and I tend to become quite withdrawn, which makes me miserable.
- I find it difficult to find the motivation to lose weight and stick to a diet plan. I get very depressed when I don't lose weight and tend to go to the other extreme and stuff myself silly.

- I resent the fact that Marie has a good figure and doesn't have to watch what she eats. I know there's nothing I can do about this.
- I resent Marie nagging me about my appearance. I admit that sometimes I over-react to what she says and just have a second helping to make a point.

Step two: my options

- I can do nothing, remain overweight and not tackle my relationship with Marie.
- I can accept my weight as it is and try and get Marie to accept me as I am.
- I can try to lose weight and persuade Marie to help me.

Step three: take the challenge

- If I don't try to lose weight, it will remain a big issue for me. I think it will stop me being the person I really want to be. I think there's also every chance that I will simply put on more weight. This won't be good for my health.
- Marie does care about me and, being a fitness freak, I don't think she'll ever accept the fact that I want to stay as I am. I think she'll continue to nag me regardless. The only option would be to keep away from her and I'd miss her company.
- If I go on a weight loss programme, I might not succeed and I might be right back where I started.
- If I ask for help from Marie, she might just laugh at me or refuse.

Step four: make a choice

- If I choose to I can change my appearance. I want to lose weight. I recognise that I may not succeed initially but I'll take that risk. I value my relationship with Marie and want her to help me. I think she's on my side. I have the right to do this my own way. If she is unwilling to help me, then I will still carry on without her.

Step five: make a gameplan

Jan decides there are two things she wants to focus on: '*1. Motivating myself to lose weight. 2. Getting Marie on my side.*'

Jan has acknowledged that she finds it difficult to motivate herself to lose weight and that she gets disillusioned very easily. She takes a practical view.

> First I will find a supervised weight loss programme. I'll ask around to see what other people recommend. I will ensure that I enrol on a programme by the end of the month. If I don't succeed, then I'll just have another go. I'll also join some exercise classes and ask Marie for help. If I lose weight then I will treat myself to some new clothes.

Jan then writes out a script to help her decide what she is going to say to her friend.

> *Marie, I want to talk to you about my decision to lose weight and I'd like to ask for your help. I know I'm overweight and I really feel very depressed about it. I also feel jealous that you can eat what you like and not put on an ounce. I know I'm sometimes over-sensitive when you comment on my appearance but, even though you may be right, I do resent you constantly telling me to do something about it. I find it incredibly difficult to motivate myself to lose weight and I feel got at when people make negative comments. I've decided to enrol in a weight loss programme. I also want to join an exercise class. I'd really appreciate your support but I do need to do this my way. Can you recommend a good fitness class and will you help me with the exercises? And please don't get out the biscuits and cakes when I come round, it just puts temptation in the way for me.*

Jan tries to imagine what her friend's response might be. She decides that if Marie laughs and tells her she'll never manage it, she will reply:

I acknowlege that it isn't easy for me to lose weight but I agree with you, I think I should try. If you help me and support me, then I am more likely to succeed. And if I don't, I'll just try again.

Jan also decides to make a pact with her friend that if she does lose weight, then both of them will treat themselves to a day at a health farm. Jan acknowledges that her weight is a big issue and whether or not she decides to deal with it, she recognises that it won't just disappear.

FOREVER AN AGONY AUNT

Margaret: *I'm having real problems with a neighbour of mine, Rita, who I've become very friendly with over the years. She's the sort of person whose life's always in a terrible state. She thinks her husband's having an affair, her kids have been in trouble with the police and she's always got something wrong with her health. The thing is, she's for ever popping in for a chat to pour out her heart to me. I've tried to be sympathetic and offer some practical advice but it doesn't seem to do much good. What's more, I'm incredibly busy and I can rarely spare the time to listen to her. I sometimes think I'll ignore the bell when she calls round, but then I feel guilty. In the end I let her in and make her coffee, but I've noticed I'm becoming much sharper with her so perhaps she'll get the message.*

There can be few people who've escaped being an unpaid agony aunt. Most of us, at some time or other, have sat up late into the night with a tearful friend, box of tissues and cups of tea at the ready. But do you sometimes wonder if your shoulder's getting a little too drenched? Are your friends and acquaintances taking advantage of your good nature and willing ear?

It's all very well acting as a municipal emotional dumping ground for all your friends, but where does it leave you? They may walk away, much the better for your tea and sympathy, and for having offloaded their problems, but are you left to pick up the emotional baggage they've left behind? And what about these people that come running to you every time they have a crisis – have they got time for you when you're in trouble? Being there for someone, in good times as well as bad, is what friendship's all about. But it's got to be a two-way effort. Attempting to act as full-time marriage counsellor, careers guidance and go-between sounds like one-way traffic. Everyone likes to feel needed. It's a great compliment that others can pour out their hearts to you. It's a powerful sensation to know that you can help people feel better. But don't be flattered into confusing your own priorities. Others may say they need you, but are they also using you?

You cannot solve the world's problems over a cup of cocoa and you can't take responsibility for sorting out someone else's life either. By all means be a good friend and be a good listener, but stand back once in a while. Set yourself a limit, let others know where you stand and make sure you have a shoulder of your own to cry on. Here's Margaret's assertive solution:

Step one: face the facts

- I like being thought of as a good friend, someone people can talk to. I find people interesting, I enjoy listening and helping them out.
- I'm getting very irritated by Rita's behaviour. She seems totally absorbed by her own needs. I don't think she's interested in helping herself.
- If I have a problem, I don't feel she listens to me. I don't think we have a two-way relationship.
- I feel angry when things that I've planned for myself have to

130

be put aside or delayed because Rita turns up. I'm cross that I let her do this.

- At the same time I don't want to feel I've let her down or deserted her.

Step two: my options

- I can do nothing and let things continue as they are in the hope that she gets the message.
- I can avoid dealing with her — not answer the bell, pretend I'm on the phone, pretend I'm going out.
- I can talk to her directly and ask her not to keep popping in.

Step three: take the challenge

- If I do nothing, I don't think she'll get the message. I'll just get more frustrated with her and more angry with myself.
- I don't think I can keep up the avoidance techniques, Rita's very persistent. I'm not a good liar and I don't think it'll work out.
- If I talk to her, she might get incredibly upset, burst into tears, accuse me of being heartless, etc, etc. She'll try to make me feel guilty. I think I might be tempted to give in, just to get her to keep quiet!

Step four: make a choice

- I cannot take responsiblity for Rita's problems. I have the right to refuse to act as Rita's shoulder to cry on, I have my own priorities and I choose to put these first. I will confront Rita openly and I'm prepared to risk our friendship becoming less close.

Step five: make a gameplan

Margaret scripts what she will say to Rita and how she might handle some of Rita's possible reactions.

> Margaret: *Rita, I know you're going through a rough patch and you've said that it's helpful to talk things through with me. But at the moment, I'm incredibly busy and I find your unplanned visits very disruptive. I admit, I was mistaken not to mention it before, but I really don't have time to spend talking to you every day. Perhaps we could make an arrangement to meet once in a while for a good chat.*
>
> Rita: *I'm really shocked, I thought you were a good friend. Good friends wouldn't say that. You can't mean it.*
>
> Margaret: *Rita, I've always been supportive towards you. I've spent many hours listening to you. But I do mean what I said. I am very busy and I find unplanned visits very disruptive. I would still like to be friends with you and I'd still like to meet, but only if we plan it in advance.*
>
> Rita: *Well, I can't see the point of continuing our friendship, if you're going to behave like this. You're the only person I can talk to. How can you do this to me?*
>
> Margaret: *I appreciate the fact that you feel you can talk to me but I cannot take responsibility for coping with your problems. I've been very supportive over the years. If you feel our friendship is over, then I regret that but I accept your decision.*

Margaret acknowledges that talking to Rita is not going to be easy and that she is going to have to be very consistent and strong in the stance she takes. Margaret feels pretty sure, that despite what she says and the tears and the recriminations on Rita's part, Rita will probably still continue to call round. Margaret decides that she won't avoid Rita but she'll say something like: 'Hallo, Rita, what can I do for you?' (in case Rita just wants a bag of sugar; she will not let Rita into the house). 'As I said to you the

*other day, I'm very busy at the moment, so I won't invite you in.
I don't have time for coffee and a chat — even a quick one. I'll
give you a call, perhaps we can get together in a couple of weeks.'*

If she says she will call Rita and arrange to meet, then
Margaret know she must do so. If she doesn't want to, then she
mustn't make any promises. At the end of the day, Margaret is
prepared to lose contact with Rita rather than go back to the
relationship they had.

BE A CONFIDENT
CONSUMER

Jinty: *I'm a really hopeless consumer. I'm one of those
people who never has the face to take anything back to the
shop when it doesn't work or breaks. I always fall for the
salesman's patter; I buy dresses and outfits that the
assistants tell me look nice, even though I'm not
convinced. I hate being pressurised so I tend to say, 'I'll
take it' just to get out of the shop. I've got a cupboard full
of useless equipment and clothes that don't quite fit. I have
tried to return things but I get so nervous. I never know
what to say and whether I'm entitled to my money back. I
think I'd be better off keeping away from the shops.*

Walk down any high street or stand in a bus queue and you'll
hear shoppers moaning and grumbling about things they've
bought which they now wished they hadn't, or goods that have
fallen apart. They swear they'll never visit the shop or buy a
particular brand again. What most of them don't do, is deal with
the situation assertively.

Consumers are flattered into buying clothes that don't suit
and utensils that are next to useless, or persuaded to make down
payments on appliances at 5.30 p.m. on the basis that they might
be sold by the next morning. Such trickery is all part of the shop
assistant's patter. It's a pity so many shoppers fall for it. Why do
we do it? Well, if you've just spent the afternoon going through

every item of clothing in your local boutique and the saleswoman says, 'Wow, that looks really stunning', it takes an assertive woman to respond, 'No it doesn't, I think I'll leave it for today.' On the whole, guilt and a desire to believe that you look a million dollars will win. Many people sign on the dotted line before they've had a chance to think things through for much the same reason. The guy's spent a whole morning trying to persuade you to buy an expensive music system, his bonus is at stake, surely it wouldn't be reasonable not to take it. Wouldn't it? It's his job to persuade you to buy, but you're under no obligation. His bonus isn't your responsibility.

And why do so many people mumble and grumble about shoddy goods and then do nothing about it? Well it's partly to do with apathy. Some consumers would rather write off the incident – and the money – than face the hassle of trekking back to the shop. Others are just too embarrassed to do anything and many people simply don't know what their legal rights are. They don't know whether they are entitled to complain and who they can complain to. As in many other situations, knowledge is power. If you know where you stand legally, who you should complain to and how you go about complaining, then you'll have more confidence to take things back and tell the shop you're dissatisfied. Your local Citizens' Advice Bureau or public library will keep a stock of leaflets from the Office of Fair Trading which will spell out your legal rights. Remember, if you want to have something put right, you need to take action immediately. You probably won't be entitled to any redress if you hang around.

If you're not bothered about your stockpile of broken and unwearable goods, then fine. If it's causing you sleepless nights, then change your shopping habits. Become an assertive consumer. Here's Jinty's assertive solution:

Step one: face the facts

- I'm easily swayed by other people's opinions. I don't have much faith in my own dress sense.
- I feel very uncomfortable confronting people. I find it difficult to say 'no'.

- I don't think I look particularly assertive. I think people take advantage of this.
- My non-assertion is costing me money.
- I've not really made an effort to find out my legal rights as a shopper. I think I'd feel more confident if I knew where I stood.

Step two: my options

- I can carry on as I am.
- I can learn to be more assertive when I'm out in the high street.

Step three: take the challenge

- If I do nothing, people will continue to take advantage of me and I'll go on wasting money. I think I'd just get depressed about it.
- If I learn to be more assertive, this will be tougher for me and I'll have to take a few risks. I'll have to be prepared to deal with the fact that I won't be every sales assistant's favourite shopper. But then again they won't throw me out of the shops or refuse to sell to me if I don't buy anything!

Step four: make a choice

- I'll choose to take the risk and learn to be more assertive when I'm out shopping. I've got much more to gain than to lose.

Step five: make a gameplan

Jinty decides she wants to concentrate on four things: '*1. I want to believe more in myself and my judgement. 2. I want to practise saying "no" to flattery. 3. I want to learn to ask for time. 4. I want to find out more about my rights and practise returning goods to shops.*'

135

She begins by making herself a personal Rights Charter.

- I have the right to know what suits me and what I want to buy.
- I have the right to listen to other people's opinions and to reject them if I think they're inappropriate.
- I have the right to have my own judgement respected.
- I have the right not to be pressurised into buying, to say 'no' and ask for time to think.
- I have the right to return goods which are broken or shoddy.

She then scripts some responses to a sales assistant's attempts to flatter her.

> Sales assistant: *That looks really great on you. The colour's wonderful.*
>
> Jinty: *Thank you. You're right about the colour but I don't feel comfortable in this dress. I'll leave it, thanks.*
>
> Sales assistant: *Are you sure? It really suits you.*
>
> Jinty: *Yes, I'm sure, thank you.*

> Sales assistant: *Why don't you try this on? It's your size, I'm sure; it's really you.*
>
> Jinty: *Let me have a look. No, I don't like it. It's not me.*
>
> Sales assistant: *Go on, just slip it on. I'm sure you'll be surprised.*
>
> Jinty: *No thanks, I don't want to try it on. I'd like to try the other skirt on.*

Next Jinty thinks about how she might deal with a sales assistant's attempts to pressurise her into buying an expensive item she's not certain about.

> Sales assistant: *Well, madam, so you'll take this washing machine.*
>
> Jinty: *I'm not sure. It's more than I wanted to spend.*
>
> Sales assistant (getting impatient): *I have spent the last two hours going through our complete range with you. This one's a bargain; you must have made up your mind by now.*

Jinty: *I appreciate the time you've spent showing me what you have, but I'm still not sure it's the right machine.*

Sales assistant: *As I said, it's an excellent offer. I can't guarantee it'll be here tomorrow.*

Jinty: *I'd like to take away the literature and have a think about it. Could you please put it aside for me and I'll call to confirm by lunchtime tomorrow.*

In situations like this, Jinty realises the sales assistant might refuse to put the item aside and she'll have to weigh up whether or not she believes it will be sold and if she can buy elsewhere if it does.

Jinty also resolves to go along to her local CAB and find out what she can do about returning faulty goods. She decides to practise the broken record technique (see page 39) and use it to take back a tin opener she bought the previous week that fell apart the first time she used it. She decides she's got to start somewhere – and it might as well be on something reasonably small!

TALK TO YOUR DOCTOR

Vicky: *I find it really difficult to talk to my GP. I always go in full of good intentions but I never say what I want to. The doctor always seems so rushed, that once I'm in the surgery I don't like to bother her. My sister's eldest child died of cot death about five years ago and that's made me really nervous about my own baby. I'm sure my GP just dismisses me as a neurotic mum whenever I turn up in the surgery – I can feel her sighing when I walk through the door, yet again. I am worried about my baby's health and I do want to talk to the GP, but how on earth do I get her to listen?*

Very many people find it especially difficult to be assertive with doctors and other members of the medical profession. Why? For a start it's extremely hard to be objective when the subject under discussion is you, your body and your health – or that of someone very close to you. You may be in pain, you may fear you have some life-threatening disease, you may be embarrassed to talk about your concerns, feel awkward about discussing personal problems or undressing in front of a stranger – even a doctor.

We tend to think of ourselves as a pretty stoic nation. We don't like to make a fuss, we'll get better if left alone and, besides, why waste the doctor's valuable time? The result – thousands of people either don't go to their doctor when they feel unwell or go into their doctor's surgery and come out without saying what they meant to. Part of this is to do with doctors' attitudes, their willingness and ability to find out what's really bothering the patient and their approach to preventive healthcare. To be fair, attitudes amongst the medical profession are changing. The old stereotype of a GP who wrote out a prescription before you got through the door, though by no means totally extinct, is at least on the way out. But this, compounded with the fact that most of us are made acutely aware, by what we read in the papers as well as what we experience ourselves, that your average neighbourhood GP or hospital consultant is under huge pressure, means that the oft-quoted phrase, 'Oh I don't like to bother my doctor' is alive and kicking, even if the patient's not too hot.

It's not stupid or daft or bothersome to be concerned about your health and wellbeing. At the very least, you have the right to be reassured that there is nothing wrong with you. You have the right to be listened to sympathetically, to be fully examined and to receive good care and medication if you need treatment.

Admittedly, it's hard to be assertive when you're lying flat on your back, semi-naked with your legs hoisted in the air – so don't try to! Choose your time carefully. Think ahead, plan what you want to ask – take a check-list of questions with you. Be an informed patient; there are plenty of books and self-help organisations around. And if you're not happy with a diagnosis, an explanation or a proposal for treatment – ask for time to think things over. After all, it's your body, it's the only one you've got. Here is Vicky's assertive solution:

138

Step one: face the facts

- My sister's experience has made me more protective towards my child than I might otherwise have been. I'm sometimes overprotective. I think I sometimes get the situation out of perspective. Other people have told me I worry too much.
- I always feel cross with myself for not confronting the doctor.
- I get tongue-tied when I'm in the surgery. I tend to be passive, I just accept what the doctor tells me. I always imagine she's just dismissing me but I've never found out how she feels. I find the fact that my GP's so rushed, and the phone's always ringing, intimidating.

Step two: my options

- I can do nothing and hope that I just grow calmer about the situation. If my baby becomes seriously ill perhaps then they'll take notice of me.
- I can change my GP.
- I can try to talk assertively to my GP and explain what my concerns are.

Step three: take the challenge

- I don't think that I'm going to worry any less about this situation and the last thing I want to happen is for my baby to get really ill. I think that just letting things go on as they are will make me more anxious and not achieve anything.
- If I change my doctor, I'd have to consult a male GP. There isn't another woman GP in my area and I'd rather see a woman.
- Although my doctor is very busy and can be abrupt when she's under pressure, I think she's basically okay. I don't think she'd laugh at me if I told her how I feel. I'd find it a big challenge to talk to her, particularly if she's in a rush with the phone going all the time.

Step four: make a choice

● I'm going to confront my doctor and explain how I feel. I'm going to ask her to give my baby a thorough examination. I have the right to feel worried about my child and the right to have those feelings respected. I have the right to be listened to.

Step five: make a gameplan

Vicky decides to concentrate on three things: '*1. I want to think about my rights and feel comfortable accepting them. 2. I'll make an appointment to see the doctor when she's least busy. I'll see if I can get one of her longer appointments. I'll talk to the receptionist and find out when's best. 3. I need to prepare what I'm going to say.*'

Vicky makes out a personal Rights Charter and spends time going over it, repeating the statements until she feels comfortable with them.

● I have the right to be worried about my child's wellbeing.
● I have the right to express my concerns.
● I have the right to have my fears recognised and accepted by others.
● I have the right to my doctor's time.
● I have the right to find that my fears are unfounded.

Then she thinks about how to approach her doctor.

I want to discuss some concerns I have about my baby's health. I find it difficult to speak to you openly and up to now I haven't been able to express how I feel. I find the fact that you are very rushed, and your phone is constantly interrupting us, intimidating.
   I know I might appear extremely anxious about my child, but my sister's baby died of cot death some years ago and I am absolutely terrified that the same thing will happen to my baby. I feel that I'm being dismissed as another neurotic

mum. I'm aware that until today I haven't explained why I'm so concerned, I didn't feel able to. I would like to be reassured that there is nothing wrong, so please could you give my baby a thorough examination. The things that are worrying me in particular are...'

Vicky also decides that she needs to know that she can call or visit her doctor at any time if she has further worries. She decides to finish their conversation by saying something like: *'I feel a lot better, now I've had the courage to talk to you. Thank you for listening to me and for examining my baby. I'd like to be able to call you or visit any time if I'm worried. The first twelve months are going to be tough for me.'*

By simply acknowledging her anxieties, both about her child and about confronting the doctor, Vicky feels more able to deal with the situation.

HANDLE THE PLUMBER

Georgia: *I recently moved into a new house and it needs quite a lot of work doing to it. I'm looking forward to having a new kitchen and bathroom — but I'm certainly not looking forward to the business of getting them put in. I hate having plumbers and fitters and decorators in the house. I feel really uneasy dealing with them. I always end up coming to blows. You never know when they're going to turn up and when they do, they create a mess or put a hole in the wrong thing. I can feel my stomach turning just at the thought of it all. How on earth am I going to get through this and keep my sanity?*

There can be few householders who don't have a similar tale of woe to tell — even if it is a bit unfair on those tradespeople who do turn up on time, clean up and do the job well. Unfortunately the reputation of the cowboys goes before them.

For many women, having a complete stranger, usually a man, traipsing through your house, banging and scraping and drilling, can be an unsettling experience. There you are, getting along quite happily, when suddenly there's an invasion of Doc Marten boots, grubby overalls, pots of noxious substances and demands for strong tea. This, together with the fact that you never know if and when the invasion will take place, makes many women want to flee their home. But dare you do it?

How can you retain control as mistress of your own home? For a start, remember that these workmen are in your house or flat, at your invitation. You're the person who hires them, who tells that what needs doing, who pays them. You have every right to know how long they will take, what the job will involve and how much they will charge. You also have the right to demand, and expect, that they look after your property and treat you, and it, with respect. Lay down the ground rules at the start. If you're not prepared to make them tea and coffee, leave the necessary utensils out and let them get on with it. If you don't want a radio playing, say so, and if you object to swearing, then ask them not to. Help yourself by moving valuable and sentimental items out of their path.

If you're not happy about the way they're carrying out the work or you sense something strange, like water running down your freshly papered walls, then shout! For some weird reason, people let builders continue to make a botch despite the fact that they thought something wasn't right at the very beginning. Don't toddle along on the basis that it might get put right; it probably won't. Ask them to stop work, point out your concern and if you don't receive a satisfactory answer, take it up with their bosses or get a second opinion. Don't pay for work you aren't satisfied with.

There can be few people who relish a visit from the building/ plumbing/wiring fraternity. Ask around for recommendations, communicate assertively and don't forget − it's your home and you're in charge! Here's Georgia's assertive solution:

Step one: face the facts

- I knew I'd have to get the builders in when I bought this house − I knew what I was in for. I have to get the work done.

- My attitude is coloured by past experiences. I haven't handled similar situations assertively. I got very het up and lost my temper. Relations with the workmen were fraught. I didn't get what I wanted.
- I'm already losing sleep over this. I can feel myself getting worked up before I've even begun.
- I'm already starting to bore my friends with my tales of woe. I think they're going to start avoiding me!

Step two: my options

I want to get the work done, so I can either:

- Carry on as before.
- Try to approach the situation more assertively.

Step three: take the challenge

- If I don't do anything, I'm likely to get a repeat of what happened before and have a thoroughly unpleasant couple of months. Even if the builders are better this time round, I probably won't appreciate them.
- If I try to approach this more assertively, I'll feel more in control. I'll be able to take any problems more in my stride and appreciate things that go well. It might be hard being firm and tough in the beginning. I'll have to learn to manage my anger more assertively, otherwise I might blow all my good intentions.

Step four: make a choice

- I accept that I'm not going to enjoy having builders in my home but I'll try to deal more assertively with the situation. I want to approach things more logically and learn to confront assertively rather than lose my temper. I also recognise that there will be a tough couple of months. I have the right to feel low and to cheer myself up with treats.

Step five: make a gameplan

Georgia wants to address two areas: '*1. I want to make a set of ground rules. 2. I want to practise confronting difficult situations and learning to manage my anger.*'

She considers what she thinks is important in order to ensure that the job is done well, to stop potential areas of disagreement and enable her to carry on her life without being completely disrupted. This is what she comes up with:

- I want a proper written quotation detailing every aspect of the work to be carried out, what will be involved, how many people there'll be and how much it will cost.
- I want an assurance of when the job will be completed and to be kept informed of any delays.
- I want to know of any extra costs before they're incurred.
- I want to know the extent of the disruption and what I need to do, clear away, etc.
- I want any mess, equipment, etc to be confined to certain agreed areas.
- I am not prepared to have loud music or swearing in the house.
- The telephone is available for necessary work calls, but I would appreciate being asked before it is used.
- I want to know to whom any complaints should be directed.

Georgia also decides to go to her local advice centre to find out what her legal rights are if something goes wrong.

Next she thinks back over some of the problems that arose in her last house and considers how she might deal with them or similar ones this time round. One incident sticks in her mind, although she hopes it won't ever happen again. She'd had a painter in to redecorate her hall and discovered that he'd got paint on her carpet. He hotly denied it was his fault and they had a blazing row over it. She thinks it over again.

Georgia: *I want to speak to you about the paint on the landing carpet...*
Decorator (interrupting): *Nothing to do with me...*

Georgia: *Please let me finish. The carpet was spotless*
   before you came to paint the hall. I'm very upset that it's
   now marked with paint. I'm going to deduct the cost of
   having it cleaned from your final bill.

Decorator: *Look, missus, it wasn't my fault, I covered the*
   carpet up. I don't see why I should lose my money.

Georgia: *I know you tried to cover the carpet up, but it*
   obviously wasn't done thoroughly enough. The carpet is
   now marked with paint and I'm not prepared to leave it
   that way. I intend to get it cleaned and I will deduct the
   cleaning charges from your final bill.

Decorator: *If you don't like the job I've done, you should*
   have said so. If you don't pay my bill, I'll take you to
   court.

Georgia: *I think the papering and painting is first class.*
   I've no complaints about your workmanship except for
   the paint marks on the carpet. Please don't threaten me. I
   am quite within my rights to ask to be compensated for
   cleaning up your paint marks on the carpet.

Georgia decides to keep a keen look-out for potential disaster
areas and tackle them before they get out of hand. Having got
her ground rules together and thought through how to approach
her builders over queries or problems, she feels more positive
about facing the situation.

FACE THE
PROFESSIONALS

Elaine: *I'm in the process of getting divorced. I've got a*
   solicitor whom my boss recommended. To start with we
   got on like a house on fire. He seemed really
   professional. He knew what he was doing and got all the
   right papers completed and what's more I felt he really
   listened to my side of the story. The last time I went to
   see him, he was quite abrupt. He didn't seem to have the

time to sit and talk to me and he just rushed through some papers I needed to sign. I'm finding the whole divorce process really stressful. I'm very worried about what's going to happen to my children. I've tried to call Mr Humphries a number of times, but he never seems available. I feel that as I'm paying what seems an awful lot of money for legal advice, I should be getting his full attention. I don't want to go off and find another solicitor. For a start I don't know of one, and what guarantee would I have that the new one would be any better?

What is it about professionals that turns normally sensible individuals into mute or gibbering globs of non-assertion? Well for a start there is the mystique — the letters after their names, the jargon, the 'uniform', the technique. It can make you feel like the only non-Brownie in a class of seven-year-olds. All the others know the password and you don't.

It doesn't matter whether people are members of a profession in the traditional sense, like solicitors, doctors and teachers, or professional technicians and craftspeople like plumbers, hairdressers or car mechanics. They all do something that you aren't equipped to do, or, you hope, can do it better than you can. Which is why you consult them in the first place. The problem with professionals such as lawyers is that you tend to come into contact with them less often than, say, your hairdresser, and when you do, there is usually more at stake. Their services also cost considerably more.

Don't get hung up on the professional mystique. Most of us are specialists in one thing or another — we have skills other members of the population don't have, we can do certain tasks better than average. We're all human beings — we eat and sleep just the same. We all have our doubts about our abilities and we all make mistakes. When you consult professionals, remember you are the client, they are your agents. They are responsible to you. You have the right to the best possible expert advice, to have your wishes respected, to be listened to. You also have the right to have mistakes rectified.

Professionals are just as responsible for communicating

146

clearly as the rest of us. Someone who's really good at a job should be able to explain the most complex technical procedure in terms a five-year-old could understand. People who say, 'I won't bother explaining, you'll never understand' usually *mean*, 'I won't bother explaining, I don't really understand it myself.' You have every right to receive a clear explanation and to ask, and ask again, until you are satisfied you understand what you have been told.

But this professional business is a two-way thing. If you're going to get the most out of your expert, you need to be a professional client. Understand what can be done for you. Don't expect the impossible, and communicate what you want clearly. Here's Elaine's assertive solution:

Step one: face the facts

- I'm very uptight about this whole divorce process. I feel very insecure at the moment, I like to feel that people are on my side. It doesn't take a lot to dent my confidence.
- I think I'm expecting my solicitor to act as a good friend, to listen to what I'm really trying to say. Maybe I'm expecting too much of him.
- I think that Mr Humphries is actually a good solicitor and he's acting in my best interests. It's his approach rather than his professionalism that's bugging me.

Step two: my options

- I can carry on and see what happens.
- I can change solicitors.
- I can try to improve the situation by talking to my solicitor.
- I can get some other professional help from a counsellor or divorce conciliator.

147

Step three: take the challenge

- This whole business is preying on my mind. I don't think ignoring it is going to make it go away. I think that if I don't deal with it, it'll just become a huge issue, another battle, out of all proportion.
- If I'm going to change solicitors that's simply going to disrupt the process. I haven't really any cause for complaint about his professionalism. I can't face the hassle of finding someone else. Better the devil you know than the devil you don't.
- If I tackle this, I think I'll feel better — I want to clear the air. Maybe he was just very rushed when I saw him, maybe it's nothing to do with my case. I haven't heard his side of the story. If ultimately I'm still not satisfied, I still have the option to change solicitors.

Step four: make a choice

- I have the right to be listened to and respected as a client. I will talk to Mr Humphries, explain my concerns and hear what he has to say. I will ignore his abrupt manner on my second visit. I think I was over-sensitive; his behaviour probably had nothing to do with me. If I'm still not satisfied after I have talked things over, then I will instruct someone else. I will also seek the support of a professional counsellor.

Step five: make a gameplan

Elaine decides that she needs to concentrate on two things, finding a counsellor, which she will do by asking around her friends and her doctor, and scripting how she is going to approach her solicitor. She concludes that she will bring up the subject at the beginning of her next meeting with Mr Humphries:

> Mr Humphries, before we start, I want to raise some concerns I have about the way I feel you're dealing with my case. I was really delighted that you took my case on. I

found your sympathetic approach and your professionalism very reassuring at our first meeting. However, whenever I've tried to contact you over the last few weeks, you are never available and none of my calls have been returned. This whole divorce process is making me very anxious, particularly what's going to happen to my children. I would like to feel I have your complete support. I would appreciate it if you could return my calls at least by the next day or get your secretary to let me know when it would be convenient to talk to you. I realise that time is money and that you are busy but I feel it's important for me to know that my case is receiving your full attention.

In fact, Elaine was right. Her solicitor had had other things on his mind on her second visit and when she mentioned it later on in the conversation, Mr Humphries apologised. He also said that he was concerned that Elaine seemed to expect him to be a sympathetic friend as well as a lawyer. Since his services were expensive and he wasn't a qualified counsellor, he didn't think it was appropriate for him to play that role. He agreed that it would be helpful if Elaine sought the expert support of a trained counsellor, and thought that it would make the legal process easier if she sorted out how she felt about things. Elaine was glad she had aired her feelings – she might well have lost a good solicitor otherwise.

ASK FOR WHAT YOU'RE WORTH

Michelle: *I'm feeling really disgruntled. I've been in my current job for well over a year now. When I joined they promised that they'd review my salary after six months. They never did. When I brought the subject up after I'd been there almost a year, my boss said he'd definitely review it when the year was up. Again nothing happened.*

I feel I'm losing out. I know business isn't that great but I think I'm doing a good job and I don't think I'm getting the recognition or the financial rewards.

Most of us like to spend money, so why do we hate asking for it — especially when we think we deserve it? Talking about money, like picking your nose in public, is generally deemed 'not nice' in the etiquette books. Because women are brought up to be nice creatures, many of us wouldn't dream of asking for a pay rise, feel awkward about stating their hourly rate or charges, and embarrassed about asking for loans to be repaid.

Acknowledging our own success is also 'not nice' in the etiquette books. We're ridiculously bashful about mentioning our achievements. We'd rather wait for someone to tell us we've done a good job, even if it means hanging on for ever, than say so ourselves. In work terms that's tantamount to falling off the career ladder at the first rung. There is a fine line between acknowledging your special skills, or a job well done, and out and out boasting which is likely to brush everyone up the wrong way. If you're pleased with what you've done, say so loud and clear. Make sure the people who matter hear about your success, don't just whisper it to the photocopy assistant.

If you want more money, ask yourself, '*Why* should my employer or my client pay me more?' Never ask for a rise just because the price of bread has gone up. Like any other job situation, do your homework first. Be prepared to sell yourself to your employer and talk about the excellent job you do; find out what the market rate is for your job; think about asking for extra perks; consider asking for promotion. Finally, if you don't think you're getting the recognition or the rewards you deserve and negotiations prove fruitless, move on. The choice is yours. This is Michelle's assertive solution:

Step one: face the facts

- I don't think the MD recognises my contribution to the company. I feel let down because my salary hasn't been reviewed as promised.

150

- I'm becoming very negative about my job. I think this is beginning to show – it won't do my prospects much good.
- I like my job. I've learnt a lot. It wouldn't be the end of the world if I left.
- If at least I could get more recognition, then I'd be a lot more satisfied.

Step two: my options

- Stay put and see what happens over the next six months.
- Make an appointment to see the MD as soon as possible, tell him what I've contributed to the company and ask for a pay rise.
- Change jobs.

Step three: take the challenge

- If I stay put, I've got no guarantee of a pay review. I'll proably feel increasingly negative and disgruntled – I might get pushed before I decide to jump.
- If I talk to the MD I might succeed in getting a rise or a promotion. At least I'll know where I stand. The worst that can happen is for them to sack me or make life so uncomfortable that I leave. I haven't worked for them for two years yet, so I'll have no come-back.
- Moving would be a bit premature. I quite like the job.

Step four: make a choice

- I think I deserve more recognition and more money. I'm going to ask for a promotion and for a rise. I'm prepared to take the risk that I might not get either and that I might even lose my job. If necessary, I'll find another job. I'm good at what I do.

Step five: make a gameplan

Michelle decides to focus on three things: '*1. I want to make a list of all my responsibilities, what I've done since I started the job and what I think I've achieved. I want to show what I've contributed to the company. 2. I want to look around and see what other people in my position are earning. I also want to see what other jobs are available. 3. I want to think about what I'm going to say to the Managing Director.*'

This is Michelle's script for confronting her MD:

> *Thank you for making the time to see me. I'd like to discuss my role in the company and how we both see it developing. I believe I've made a very positive contribution to the company over the past year. I was particularly pleased with the success of...* (Michelle outlines two specific projects and shows how her work benefited the company). *As you are aware, I have been shouldering increasing amounts of responsibility. For example* (she talks about new responsibilities that she's taken on since she started the job and how well she's handled them). *When I took on this job, I was promised a salary review after six months. I discussed this with you at the time, and you then agreed to review it when I'd been with the company a year. I've now been here fifteen months. I don't believe that my current position and my salary reflect the high quality of my work and the increasing responsibilities I am taking on. I would like to discuss with you promotion to a more senior level and of course an increase in salary. I feel this move would recognise my contribution more accurately.*

Michelle knows the MD's habits quite well by now and considers how he might respond. He's well known for hedging.

> MD: *Yes, well, Michelle, we're very pleased with your performance but I can't really comment on a promotion at the moment. You know we've been going through a bad patch, I couldn't commit us to any changes right now.*

Michelle: *I understand that business isn't strong at the moment. But I'd still like to know where I stand. You say you're pleased with my performance. I think I've made a positive contribution to the company and I no longer feel my current position or salary reflect my new responsibilities. I'd want to know whether you would be able to consider a promotion within the next three to four months and what sort of salary increase I could expect.*

On the basis of the MD's reply Michelle will make a decision whether to stay with the company and see what happens or start looking for another job immediately. Michelle decides that if the MD can't give her a fixed time for her review, then she will leave in any case within four months if nothing happens. In the meantime she signs on with a recruitment agency, just to keep her options open.

PUT PAID TO WORK OVERLOAD

Laura: *I'm a history teacher at my local comprehensive. Because I enjoy sport, I also do some extra athletics coaching for the younger pupils. I suppose it's my own fault — I'm conscientious and keen and I get landed with all sorts of extra-curricular activities. The headteacher has now asked me whether I'd consider putting on a special end of term show. Initially I leapt at the opportunity but I've realised that with exam marking and the school sports day I might just end up with a nervous breakdown. I don't see how I can get out of it now I've committed myself.*

Own up, are you the sort of person who always gets landed with the dud jobs no one else wants or the meetings that interfere with someone else's plans for a quiet evening in front of their TV? Is your desk a paper mountain and your diary full of logistically impossible engagements? Are you a victim of work overload?

When you fall into the trap of accepting too much work, either work that really isn't your responsibility or assignments you cannot reasonably be expected to complete within a deadline, then one of two things can happen. You either get the job done, in which case everyone thinks how wonderful and capable you are and therefore piles on even more, or you turn into a jittering bag of nerves, in which case you can wave goodbye to your reputation as an effective worker. Why do we go on accepting tasks and responsibilities that push us beyond our limits? There are a number of reasons. First, if you want to prove yourself, it's difficult to say 'no' to a job that might give you a chance to shine. Secondly, if you're keen and enthusiastic about a particular project, it's easy to imagine that somewhere along the line you will find time to do it. Thirdly, the work culture teaches us to play the game and not let the side down; we're taught to take what's thrown at us, especially if it's by someone older or more senior. Finally, there are those who simply cannot say no.

Of course, there is the argument that you don't know what you can achieve until you're pushed. That's all very well, but you can only be pushed to the outside edge once in a while; for most of us that's not the healthiest place to exist on a daily basis. If you don't learn to say 'no' and take the risk that you might offend a colleague, or that your superworker reputation might be momentarily dented, you may find yourself unable to work effectively at all. (For more information on assertive time management, look at pages 168–172). Here's Laura's assertive solution:

Step one: face the facts

- I enjoy my job, I'm keen to do everything and do it well.
- I'm ambitious, I want to make a good impression and show others how committed I am.
- I find it hard to turn requests down. As a result I've usually got too much on my plate.
- I'm worried that if I refuse to do something, the staff and headteacher or the kids will think less of me.
- I feel others take advantage of my enthusiasm.

Step two: my options

- I can go ahead with both the show and the sports day — and the exam marking; it'll only be for another couple of months and I'll have the summer holidays to recover.
- I can go and see the head and say that I'm prepared to take responsibility for either the sports day or the end of term show but not both.

Step three: take the challenge

- If I go ahead with everything I'm going to get overstressed and I'll end up chasing my tail and being ratty. Knowing me, I'll probably be really busy over the summer so I won't get a chance to rest. If I don't say anything then next year the problems will probably start all over again.
- If I make a choice I'll feel as if I've let myself and the others down. The head might take a slightly dimmer view of me. Someone else will get the fun and the kudos of organising the sports day or the end of term show.

Step four: make a choice

- I'm prepared to admit that I made a mistake and risk others being disappointed, but I'd prefer to take on only one major activity. I don't mind which. I feel if I don't make my stand now, the overload will just continue.

Step five: make a gameplan

Laura decides to confront the headteacher as soon as possible and tell him of her decision. She also wants to practise learning to say 'no'. She scripts what she wants to say to the head.

The other day you asked me if I would put on the end of term show. I was very flattered to be asked and I agreed.

155

Now I've had a chance to think it over, I realise that I made a mistake. I feel that I cannot take on the show as well as all my other commitments such as the sports day, and do them well. I'm more than happy to organise either the sports day or the show, but not both. Which would you rather I took on?'

Laura considers how the head might respond.

Head: *Laura, I wish you'd said this last week. I'm relying on you to put on the end of term show, you're really the only one who can get the whole thing together.*

Laura: *I'm sorry, I admit I made a mistake, I should have asked for time to think it over. I'm quite prepared to take on the show providing someone else organises the sports day.*

Head: *Look, I'm sure you can take both things on – we don't want anything elaborate. Why don't you start and we can see how things go?*

Laura: *I'm flattered that you think I can undertake both the sports day and the show but to do either of them properly I need to devote time to it. I'm not prepared to start both projects and see how things go. Which would you prefer me to take on?*

Laura also thinks back to when the head originally asked her to take on the end of term show. She practises responding more assertively:

Thank you for asking me. It sounds very exciting but I have a lot of other commitments and I'd like some time to think your offer over.

By admitting to herself that she can be over-enthusiastic, Laura finds it easier to come to terms with the fact that she will have to learn to say 'no' more often. However she reminds herself that taking on fewer demands doesn't actually mean she's any less committed – just more rational about deciding how she uses her time.

CONFRONT SEXUAL HARASSMENT

Barbara: *I've been working for my current firm for about five years. I like the job but I don't like the man I now have to work for. He's a real old lecher. Every time he asks me to do something, he puts his arm round me or pats my knee. He's forever telling me blue jokes and about what a Casanova he is. His whole attitude and his behaviour make me feel physically sick but I don't know whether I should say anything to him or to the Managing Director. I doubt whether the other women who've worked with him before said anything. Maybe I'm just being prudish.*

Over the past few years the sordid issue of sexual harassment has raised its public profile considerably. It's not just a workplace hazard. Sexual harassment can occur anywhere, whether it's an overt wolf whistle on the street, fondling on a crowded train or more insidious, long-term power games in the office that ultimately cost someone their job.

The majority of victims of sexual harassment are women, but men can be equally vulnerable. Age, position, looks are immaterial. What counts is that the harasser usually has power over his or her victim. It may be the boss, the landlord, the college tutor or simply a bigger and stronger person. So what constitutes sexual harassment? It includes: unnecessary and persistent touching or other unwanted physical contact; verbal abuse, suggestive comments and jokes; pestering for sexual favours or compromising invitations; pin-ups or other offensive displays; and ultimately sexual assault and rape. But, the pub bar argument goes, some people are so prudish, it's only a bit of harmless fun. Where do you draw the line between innocuous flirting and sexual harassment? What matters is that you, as an individual, find the behaviour unacceptable, regardless of what anyone else feels.

157

So why do so many women put up with sexual harassment? For a start some wonder if they've been imagining the whole thing. They feel they may have misconstrued a remark or convince themselves the train is overcrowded and the man simply overbalanced. This is perhaps the hardest part, recognising and coming to terms with the fact that you are being harassed. Then there is the problem of power. Many people are simply too frightened to complain. They worry that they might lose their job or jeopardise their career prospects.

There's no point in pretending that acknowledging and dealing with sexual harassment is going to be easy. You will need to use all your assertion skills and all your courage to confront your harasser. Remember that, with growing awareness about sexual harassment, companies are far more aware of the problem, and that ultimately the law offers some protection. Here's Barbara's assertive solution:

Step one: face the facts

- My boss is sexually harassing me.
- I like my job but I'm beginning to dread coming in in the morning. My boss's behaviour is affecting my health.
- I feel angry that he's affecting my enjoyment of my work.
- I have no idea whether other women who have worked with him feel the same way as I do.
- I'm worried that other people will think I'm prudish and making an unnecessary fuss.

Step two: my options

- I could grin and bear it, try to avoid him and give him the cold shoulder. Perhaps he'll get the message.
- I could confront him, tell him how I feel and ask him to stop.
- I could take the matter up with the MD.
- I could look for another job.

Step three: take the challenge

- If I do nothing at least I won't rock the boat, but I have no guarantee he'll get the message. If he doesn't the situation may just escalate. I don't think I could carry on with my job. I'd probably resign.
- If I confront him he may ignore me or become aggressive. It might be just as impossible to carry on working for him.
- My MD might not believe me.
- I don't really want to look for another job. If I quit I'll feel he has won.

Step four: make a choice

- I'm not prepared to go on being miserable. I have the right to go to work without being harassed. I have the right to say how I feel and to be respected. I will confront my boss and if necessary take the matter up with the MD. I have the right to enjoy my job. Ultimately I'm prepared to take legal advice and if appropriate leave the company.

Step five: make a gameplan

Barbara has six points in her gameplan: '*1. I will keep a diary of my boss's comments and actions as evidence. 2. I want to talk to the other women. 3. I will confront my boss. 4. I will talk to the MD. 5. I will seek legal advice. 6. I want to be ready to confront harassment in the future.*'

Barbara realises that it's important to get together evidence of the way her boss is sexually harassing her, especially if she has to embark on legal proceedings. She also needs to let other people know how she feels. By talking to the other women she discovers that many of them had had similar experiences and were quite relieved to be able to discuss them openly. However, all were reluctant to take the matter up either with Barbara's boss or the MD. They all said they would wait and see how Barbara got on.

Barbara then scripts what she wants to say to her boss. She also decides to put her complaint in writing and, depending on the outcome of the meeting, send a copy of her letter to the MD. This is what Barbara scripts:

I want to discuss the way you have been treating me. I find your behaviour threatening and it makes me feel extremely uncomfortable. In particular I don't like the way you put your arm around me and pat my knee. I find this physical contact unnecessary and demeaning. In addition I resent having to listen to your sexual jokes and your claims about your sexual prowess. I don't believe these remarks are appropriate for the office. Please will you stop this behaviour as it is sexual harassment.

She then considers some of the responses she might get.

Boss: *Oh come on Barbara, we're both adults. What's all this, the wrong time of the month, eh?*

Barbara: *I find that last comment unnecessary. I realise I should have spoken about this before, but I didn't and I'm discussing it now. I am aware that we are both adults, that's why I am telling you that I object to the physical contact, sexual innuendo and remarks. Please will you stop sexually harassing me.*

Boss: *So you're accusing me of sexual harassment? Well I'm your boss, what are you going to do about it? Resign?*

Barbara: *Yes, I do feel you are sexually harassing me but no, I will not be bullied into resigning. I shall be taking the matter up with the Managing Director.*

Boss: *Well, he's not likely to believe you.*

Barbara: *We shall see. Other women in the company feel the same way as I do and have had similar experiences. If necessary I shall get legal advice before I decide what further steps to take.*

Barbara then prepares a similar script with which to confront the MD. In the meantime she decides to take some informal legal advice from a lawyer friend to find out how the law protects her. Finally she realises that even though she may have put a stop to this instance of sexual harassment, another one might arise somewhere else. She thinks back to how she could have tackled the problem when it first arose. She considers three situations:

Responding to her boss putting his arm around her:
'Please don't put your arm around me. I don't like it and I find it totally unnecessary.'

Responding to her boss beginning to tell a dirty joke:
'I suggest that you don't continue with the joke. I find those sort of jokes extremely offensive and inappropriate in the office.'

Responding to an invitation to dinner:
'Thank you for the invitation, but I prefer to keep my business and social lives quite separate. I'm sure that we can make time to discuss whatever it is you want to during office hours.'

Barbara resolves to tackle sexual harassment head on if it ever occurs again.

7

Looking Good, Feeling Good

Style and charisma — many people spend hundreds of pounds attempting to capture those elusive qualities. The fact is, they're not for sale. Flair and charm, call them what you will, are not to be found on cosmetics counters and clothes hangers. The magic glow comes from within. Confidence is more than skin deep. Believing in yourself is what counts ... but as we said earlier, it doesn't do any harm to enhance what you've got!

These short sections aren't intended as a comprehensive style guide, they simply offer some straightforward advice to help you make the most of your best features and camouflage the ones you like least. When you *know* you look good, you feel good about yourself. Having confidence in your appearance is a big boost to your overall sense of self worth.

Most of us know instinctively what does and doesn't suit us. The problem is, the desire and temptation to snap up a bargain, dress convention and misguided advice sometimes lead us astray. You know you've got it right when you walk out of the house and someone says, 'Wow, you look great'. You know you've got it wrong when you feel perfectly fine and a friend asks you, 'Are you okay, you look terribly tired?' How can you get it right most of the time?

CLOTHES

Here are the top five tips:

1 *Wear colours that make you glow*

Open up your wardrobe, what do you see? If you're confronted with a rainbow from bright fuchsia pink to dusky blue, murky brown to lime green, the bet is, you don't wear half your clothes!

Learn to recognise which colours suit you. Remember that for every primary colour, as well as black and white, there are very many different shades. So while burgundy might make you look like death warmed up, salmon pink may well look stunning. Go along to the silk scarf or sweater department of your local store and hold up the colours against your face. Try to draw together a collection that suits you — colours that make your eyes glow, that give your skin a healthy sheen not a sickly pallor. If you've got them right you should find that all the colours blend together harmoniously.

2 *Don't fall into the black trap*

There is a tendency, especially among women who have to wear suits to work, to believe that professional clothing should be either black or dark navy. The fact is that very few people can actually wear these colours near their face without eliciting concerned enquiries about the state of their health. Find an alternative shade that enhances you, pewter perhaps or olive green, a golden brown or something brighter. You'll look far more successful in a less standard colour that enhances you than in traditional black or dark navy which doesn't. In the same way, check out your blouses. If you've got both brilliant white and creamy ivory on your shelves, then one of them must go because they can't both suit you. Try them both on. Is one more flattering to your skin tone and hair colouring than the other? Try out some brighter colours to go with your sombre suit too. Set aside some time to experiment. Wear the suit when you next go clothes shopping and try it on with different coloured tops. Try new colours that you haven't considered before. You could take along a friend to give you honest advice on which colours look good.

3 *Accentuate your best features and flatter the rest*

Treat your body with respect. Play up your favourite features and be kind to the others. Here are some basic dos and don'ts.

Height: If you're tall, avoid small prints and dainty accessories, go for bold. If you're petite, keep it simple.

Legs: If your legs are heavy, avoid short skirts and hosiery that isn't plain and on the darker side. Wear shoes with a slight heel rather than flat ones. If you've got skinny legs then again avoid short skirts and certainly stilettos, unless you want to look like a beanpole. Try lighter coloured, but not constrasting, tights to make your legs look fuller. For short legs, keep well away from long or full skirts and trousers. Go for the shorter skirt, shorts, cropped trousers and short jackets.

Hips, bottom and thighs: If you're worried about the width of your hips, don't go anywhere near full gathered skirts or clothes with details such as pockets on the hips. Try skirts with centre seams or slight pleating at the front of the waistband, and jackets that don't stop on your hips. If your bottom's broad, avoid straight tight skirts, shorts and trousers, go instead for loose (not full) gathered skirts and longer jackets. Concentrate on your top half. The same applies if you've got heavy thighs; you don't want short skirts or shorts, but why not try culottes?

Bust: If you'd like more than you've got, avoid clingy tops with plunging necklines and go for loose blouses and shirts with lots of details and interesting patterns. If you're more than well endowed, then try the opposite: avoid fussy or high necklines, try open and V-necklines, use shoulder pads and also drop waistlines.

Balancing torso and legs: If your waist is up somewhere near your bust, then you probably feel uncomfortable wearing belts. Give yourself a longer look by avoiding cropped jackets and high-waisted skirts and trousers, try instead longer jackets, overblouses and drop-waisted dresses. On the other hand, if you've more body than leg, go for short or cropped jackets and if your waist can take it, wide belts.

4 *Don't be a fashion victim*

The cat-walks of Paris and Milan and the pages of *Vogue* are intended only for inspiration — unless you're a pre-pubescent model and/or extremely rich. Being fashionable does not mean wearing the latest trend. It means wearing a variation of the current trend — one that makes the best of what you've got. If the fashion is for shorter skirts then wear them where they flatter you most, whether it's above, on or just below the knee.

This is terribly boring advice but unfortunately it's true: rather buy a couple of expensive items that are well cut, well made and classic than a host of trashy ones. To discover the real cost of your wardrobe, divide the price you paid for each piece by the number of times you've worn it. You may find that your £200 jacket is actually better value than the one you bought for £50. Use the sales to buy better clothes that are reduced to the price you would have paid for a similar item out of the sale.

5 *Look the part*

What sort of image do you project? Are your clothes sending out the same message as your brain? Think about your role, particularly if you're about to return to work. That dress may be pretty but does it mean business? By all means use a hint of a frill to give a more feminine look but watch out for tweeness. Does your cardigan look smart or does it look sloppy? Be careful your sharp suit isn't a turn-off, particularly if you're in a caring profession. Be comfortable but be appropriate.

MAKE-UP

You may be reluctant to cover your face with paints and potions, but like everything else make-up is an important part of your total image. If you are taking care over the clothes you choose to wear and how you dress your body, you also need to think about how you dress your face. Just as clothes need to be appropriate to the situation, so does make-up.

So, if you put on your best suit and smartest shoes for a job interview, but leave the face bare, the impression you give is that you are only half dressed and not fully committed.

This doesn't have to mean the full works, but some well-applied foundation, a little colour and lipstick will make all the difference.

And remember that make-up, like hemlines, changes according to the current fashion. Make sure your face does not get left behind.

These days it's not difficult to get information and advice about skin care and make-up. A trip to the cosmetics counter of your local store or a visit to a beauty salon will provide you with plenty of useful know-how. Here are the basics for make-up with staying power.

1 Use a good concealer, a shade lighter than your foundation to hide stray spots, dark lines and blemishes. Apply before foundation and also touch up after.

2 Don't skip foundation, otherwise the rest of your make-up will sink without a trace before you're even out of the door. If you really don't like it, try a tinted moisturiser. Remember to stroke the foundation on downwards, preferably on a damp cosmetic sponge, gliding over your pores not into them.

3 Brush all over with a translucent powder. This is your 'fix'. If your skin tends to be oily, press the powder on with a powder puff first and then brush off the excess.

4 Now put some colour on your eyes. Keep it subtle and avoid pearly colours during the day. First put a base colour over the whole eye area, then light brush a slightly darker shade over the outside half. If you want to use an eyeliner, try a soft kohl pencil. Only ever outline the outer third of your top and bottom lids — this will give you a wider-eyed look. Finish off with some mascara and give your eyebrows a quick brush out.

5 Next apply blusher. Use a big fluffy brush to make it look more professional. Use short, light strokes along the base of your cheek bone (suck your cheeks in), starting at the hairline and working inwards. Watch you don't go too far into the centre of your face.

6 Use a special pencil to outline the shape of your lips and fill in using a lip brush loaded with colour from your favourite lipstick.

This way you'll get much more definite and long-lasting colour than by applying the lipstick directly.

Keep some powder and lipstick handy to touch up during the day. By night experiment with something more dramatic.

Watch what your spend on cosmetics. Go for fewer, better quality products, they'll have better staying power and will probably be less irritant. If your skin tends to be a problem, consider cutting down on camouflage materials and go for a regular facial instead.

HAIR

Is yours your crowning glory or a haystack with a will of its own? If you've worn the same hairstyle for the last twenty years, ask yourself if it isn't time to take the plunge and get it restyled. It doesn't take much to bring hair up to date.

Get a hairdresser that you trust and stick to them. Look for people whose hair you admire and ask them where they get it done. There's little substitute for keeping hair in good condition and having regular cuts. Always get a style you can manage. Better something less glamorous that you can rinse and run with in the mornings than a fabulous hairdo only your hairdresser can achieve. If you have any kind of treatment such as a perm or colour, remember your hair will need extra care to keep it looking good – and don't forget to have your roots retouched!

BODY

Look after your body, it's the only one you've got! Eating balanced, regular meals, getting sufficient sleep and taking appropriate exercise are part and parcel of feeling good both physically and mentally. If your life is running you, leaving you little time to eat and sleep properly, then get off the treadmill.

Take a good look at your habits. Do you:

● Spend your mealtimes bouncing up from your chair to serve others?

- Serve yourself less or inferior food to others in your family
- Grab hurried snacks as you rush around the home or office?
- Go to bed later or get up earlier to do things for others that they could do for themselves?
- Not exercise because you haven't time or don't think you'd succeed?

If the answer to any of the above is 'yes', then use your assertion skills to make the time to sit down, enjoy and digest your food, and get your required quota of rest and exercise. *Remember your assertion rights*.

Finally, take your health seriously, make it a priority. Take advantage of regular health screening. Don't be afraid of seeking help if you're worried about a lump or pain or some discomfort. If it turns out to be nothing, great, if there's something wrong, then ignoring it won't make it go away. Regular check ups will also put paid to hypochondriacal worrying – which is a complete waste of energy!

Help yourself to health by not poisoning your body with substances like cigarettes and alcohol. An occasional social drink never did anyone any harm but if it's getting out of hand, be assertive, seek help. Smoking, however, is an addiction whether it's one or fifty cigarettes a day. Get professional advice on how to kick the habit.

Manage your time

Are you one of the many women for whom combining demanding roles of worker, housekeeper, mother and partner means you spend your life feeling like a hamster on an ever turning tread-wheel? Do you ever sense that even if you were to deprive yourself of sleep for a week you'd still never complete everything you have to do? Too much to do and too little time to do it in is one of the biggest causes of frustration, exhaustion and overstress, with all the complications and damaging effects that those three can lead to. How can you help yourself to manage your time more effectively and cut out the unnecessary stress?

168

For a start, remember that superwoman is not assertive. You cannot do everything and be all things to people – and do it well. Have a good look at the way you spent your days. How much of your energy is spent doing things which you believe are worthwhile and positive – and how many of your activities leave you feeling drained and undervalued? Maybe it's time to overhaul what you do with your hours and put your priorities into perspective. Here's a ten-point Assertive Time Plan to help you at home and work.

Assertive time plan

1 *Be realistic about your time*
There's no point in taking on so many tasks that you're forced to complete some of them at 2 a.m. when you're probably not at your best. Be realistic about the time it takes to carry out essential tasks like shopping, eating, washing. Think about how much sleep you need each night to function properly the next day. If you have young children and are dogged by sleepless nights, be sensible about what you commit yourself to. Also learn to recognise during which parts of the day you are most alert. Are you an early bird or a night owl?

2 *Practise saying 'no'*
Ask yourself, 'Have I the time to take on this request, complete it well and still have sufficient time to carry out the other things I want to do?' Look back over pages 153–156.

3 *Make daily 'to do' lists*
Instead of letting a hundred and one tasks swirl around in your mind in an uncoordinated muddle, put them all down on paper. Include all the niggling things that have been lurking in the back of your head for far too long – dental appointments, calls to long-lost friends, a visit to the dry cleaners. When you've got them all in black and white, start putting them in order of priority. It's always worth trying to tackle the biggest tasks first and leaving the smaller ones as fillers for when you're feeling less on the ball. It also helps if you get the ones you most loathe

out of the way at the start — the rest will then seem like plain sailing.

Review your list each evening — it gives a great sense of satisfaction to see all those tasks crossed off. Watch that your lists don't become unrealistic. To repaint your house, write your first novel and do the Christmas shopping in one day, or even a week, is hardly achievable. Don't set yourself an impossible goal.

4 *Learn to delegate*

Don't fall into the trap of thinking you're the only one who can do the job. Learn to delegate responsibilities to others — colleagues, partners, children, paid help. Accept that other people may not carry out the work in exactly the same way as you or perhaps with similar skill and care. Ask yourself whether that really matters so long as the job gets done and you stay ahead of your workload. Have a look back over Making Requests, pages 37–40.

5 *Create quiet thinking time*

We all need a quiet time during the day, whether it's to do some detailed work, to plan activities or simply to reflect. Tell other people when your quiet time is, make it clear you don't want to be disturbed, lock the door if necessary and switch on the answering machine. Under no circumstances agree to see or speak to others during your quiet time — unless you want to. If you keep a regular quiet hour (or two) others will come to respect it.

6 *Don't delay*

Don't put off until tomorrow what you can do today. The longer you procrastinate, the more of a mountain the task will seem. Reply to telephone calls and letters while they're fresh in your mind. Get your tasks out of the way.

7 *Don't try for perfection*

This doesn't mean that you go ahead and carry out what you need to do any old how. It does mean not driving yourself into a hole in the ground in a desperate attempt to dot every i and cross every t. Of course some jobs need to be done with meticulous care, but on the whole you can step back and ask yourself, 'Is this okay given the time I've had to do it in and everything else I need to complete?'

All of us do some things better than others – if you can turn out a soufflé at the drop of a hat, great, if you can't, keep your dinner parties simple. Concentrate on what you're good at, find an easy way out of the rest.

8 *Make use of gadgets*

Today's domestic appliances and office equipment would leave our grandmothers astounded, and no doubt envious. Don't shun modern gadgets, every good time manager needs them. Washing machines, dishwashers, food processors, convenience foods – use them. When you're baking fresh bread and concocting homemade soups and cakes in the dawn hours, ask yourself, 'Okay, this is all very commendable for our diets, but what's this routine doing for my health?' Ease up, get a takeaway once in a while!

A word about telephone answering machines. You may scorn them but they're invaluable in helping you to take control over your time. Use them to screen unwanted interruptions and deal with other people's demands at your convenience.

9 *Cut out the dead wood*

Have a good clear out! Throw out the clothes that don't fit, the cleaning materials that you don't use, the strange lumps in the freezer you're never going to eat, the old papers in your desk drawer. Watch that you don't accumulate more rubbish. Read a magazine, cut out the article you want to keep and bin the rest. Be honest about your friends and acquaintances. Stop keeping in contact with the ones that drain you, the ones that always want and never give. See pages 129–133.

10 *Make time for yourself*

Any 'to do' list that doesn't include time for yourself, whether it's for a favourite hobby or a chance to read a book, simply won't work. You're not a mechanical engine running for the benefit of others; take time to recharge your batteries. Schedule into your day some time, even if it's only half an hour, to spend just on you – bedtime doesn't count. This might come as a shock to those around you but it's a reminder that every one of us has to recognise her own needs (see below).

RELAX!

The more tense and wound up you become, the more difficult it is to relax. For this reason, finding the means to switch off on a daily basis is important. The penalties for failing to relax are well documented. People who are overstressed suffer all sorts of ill effects, their behaviour changes, they may become short-tempered or start smoking or drinking, sleeplessness – or the desire to sleep – are common, as are physical complaints such as stomach upsets, headaches and so on.

Learn to recognise the symptoms of being overstressed and with the help of your assertion skills, take some positive steps to get back to being your real self.

Switch off

What do you do to switch off? Go shopping? Garden? Watch TV? Take a bath? Switching off, making time for ourselves, doing things that are only for our own benefit has two purposes. First, it's a means of getting out of the rat race, of relaxing away from our usual routine, and secondly, it's a way of pampering ourselves. Being good to yourself should become part of your daily schedule. Don't just reserve treats for when you've achieved something outstanding, reward yourself regularly when you know you've tried hard. And on those days when you think, to heck with the world, go on, be nice to yourself.

Switching off need be neither elaborate nor expensive. What matters is that it gives you pleasure and a sense of satisfaction. And remember, you don't have to justify it to anyone. Here's a selection of ideas:

- **Take a bath!** Well not quite, make it special. Gather all your pots and potions, oils and creams plus a cassette recorder or radio and a scented candle. Lock the bathroom door – if you have to – run yourself a deep warm bath, pour in your favourite bath oil, put a match to the candle, turn on your most soothing music and switch off the main bathroom light. Then indulge!

  For a variation on the bathing theme why not make an appointment with your local beauty salon for a facial, massage or some other treatment – it need not be expensive. If you want to splash out try a day or a weekend at a health club.

- **Exercise your brain.** Keep your mind alert. Go to bed early with a book or the daily papers, join a library, sign up for a course at your local adult education college. Doing something, such as a course, on a regular basis may be an excellent way of breaking away from your usual routine. Try your hand at a new hobby or revive an old passion. Be creative! Treat yourself to new equipment or materials and make the time and space to carry out your craft.

- **Exercise your body.** Go for a walk or make a regular swimming date. Or even take up aerobics or windsurfing, or join a dance class. Get your metabolism going and feel good about yourself.

- **Food's a great relaxer.** If your enjoy cooking but don't usually get a chance to do it, shut yourself in the kitchen for an afternoon and prepare something really special. If you can't wait to get away from the kitchen sink, then why not treat yourself to dinner out or invest in a range of upmarket ready prepared meals and put your feet up for the evening? Turn an ordinary shopping trip into a treat by having lunch or tea at your favourite eating place.

- **Socialise.** If you don't normally get a chance to sit and chat, why not set up a regular 'date'? This arrangement works equally well with long-standing spouses as with a girls' night out. Friends are important, make time to see them.

  Plan special trips. Doing things on the spur of the moment can be fun but why not plan ahead and look forward to something special? Take a day out in the country – or in

173

town. Think about what you want to see, search out somewhere good to eat, take along your favourite people.
- **Make birthdays and anniversaries a real treat**. Even if your friends and partner forget your special day, plan to make it the highlight of your week. Spoil yourself! Make every day a birthday!

From Here Onwards

There's no magic formula to becoming assertive. It takes courage, will-power and perhaps a little inspiration to change lifelong habits. It also takes time.

Accepting that you have the right to be yourself and take responsibility for your life is not like beginning and ending a school lesson. The learning curve goes on forever. None of our lives are ever static — even discovering you're in a rut brings a new challenge. Greet every achievement with enthusiasm. Treat every set-back — and there will be some — as a valuable experience from which to grow and find the strength to deal with the next challenge.

The tips and advice in this book are only a beginning, a way-mark. They're not intended as an instant sticky plaster cure all to patch up a damaged ego scarred over many years. However small or great the knocks that have hammered at your self esteem, the power to heal them must ultimately come from within you.

Right at the beginning of the book you were asked to identify your dreams and fantasies. Perhaps that was an impossible request as you no longer had the optimism to dream. Maybe now you can set your imagination free. Remember those dreams. Recall how good it felt to be inside them. But don't just leave your fantasies in dream land, bring them into the real world. Think of them as goals — concrete objectives to aim for and achieve. And even if in the end you never quite grasp those goals, think how much more you've gained from the game of life as you travelled towards them.

No one is powerless. In at least some small way we can all control our lives, make opportunities work for us, expand our horizons, and stand up for what we think. Learn to believe in yourself and the glass prison will always crack. It's your life. Choose how you live it.

Index

PIATKUS BOOKS

Now you have read *The Right to be Yourself* you may be interested in the following titles, all published by Piatkus Books.

Assertive talk and public speaking

Confident Conversation: How to talk in any business or social situation   Dr Lillian Glass
He Says, She Says: Closing the communication gap between the sexes   Dr Lillian Glass
Powerspeak: The complete guide to public speaking and presentation   Dorothy Leeds
The Power Talk System: How to communicate effectively Christian H. Godefroy and Stephanie Barrat

Interviews and careers

Marketing Yourself: How to sell yourself and get the jobs you've always wanted   Dorothy Leeds
Networking and Mentoring: A woman's guide   Dr Lily M. Segerman-Peck
Personal Power: How to achieve influence and success in your professional life   Philippa Davis
The Influential Woman: How to achieve success without losing your femininity   Lee Bryce
Which Way Now? How to plan and develop a successful career Bridget Wright

Looking good

Colour Me Beautiful: Discover your natural beauty through colour   Carole Jackson
The Colour Me Beautiful Make-Up Book   Carole Jackson
The Complete Style Guide from The Color Me Beautiful Organisation   Mary Spillane

The Colour and Style File: Enjoy a wardrobe that works for you   Barbara Jacques
Wardrobe: Develop your style and confidence   Susie Faux with Philippa Davis

Relaxation

Super Massage: Simple techniques for instant relaxation Gordon Inkeles
The Three Minute Meditator: 30 simple ways to relax and unwind   David Harp

Self-protection

Protect Yourself: How to be safe on the streets, in the home, at work, when travelling   Jessica Davies

Sex

Becoming Orgasmic: A sexual and personal growth programme for women   Julia R. Heiman and Joseph LoPiccolo
Good Vibrations: The Complete Guide to sex aids and erotic toys
Suzie Hayman

For a free brochure with further information on our complete range of titles, please write to:

Piatkus Books
5 Windmill Street
London, W1P 1HF

PIATKUS